HEBREWS

by Donnie V. Rader

ONESTONE
BIBLICAL RESOURCES

Published by:
One Stone Press
979 Lovers Lane
Bowling Green, KY 42103

Printed in the United States of America

ISBN (10 Digit): 1-94142-212-8
ISBN (13 Digit): 978-1-94142-212-8-0

Supplemental Materials Available:
PowerPoint slides for each lesson
Answer key
Downloadable PDF

Table of Contents

Introduction To The Book Of Hebrews

A thorough study of the book of Hebrews can be an intimidating task for some. The depth of the book causes some to wonder why we need to study such a book. However, those who feel this way need the book more than they realize.

If you need encouragement, you need the book of Hebrews. If you need Christ (who is better than prophets, angels, Moses, and Aaron), you need the book of Hebrews. If you need to be reminded to not give up, but keep pressing on to the end, you need the book of Hebrews. If you need to hear about the dangers of falling back, you need the book of Hebrews.

Though there is depth, the message is quite simple. It is designed to exhort (Heb. 13:22).

The Title

The English text. The English text has the title, "The Epistle to the Hebrews."

The Early Manuscripts. The early manuscripts bear the title "to Hebrews."[1] "But this much is certain, that the title was prefixed to our epistle at a very early date, and most likely before the close of the Apostolic age."[2] It was later enlarged to read "the Epistle to the Hebrews.[3]

The name "Hebrew." This term was first used in Genesis 14:13. Its use here (and rest of the Old Testament) emphasized a foreigner. "And hence the name Hebrew is commonly used whenever foreigners are introduced as the speakers; or when the Israelites are speaking of themselves to foreigners; or when they are in any way contrasted with foreigners."[4] It was used in the Old Testament to denote all the descendants of Jacob. It came to denote those who spoke the Hebrew language. In the New Testament, "the name 'Hebrew' seems to have always some reference to the language, as well as the many other rights and privileges of the seed of Abraham."[5]

Thus, this was written for a Jewish audience.

---

1   Manuscripts Aleph, A, and B. See Daniel H. King, Sr., *The Book of Hebrews*, Truth Commentaries, 11.

2   Robert Milligan, *Vol. IX – Epistle to the Hebrews*, New Testament Commentary, 27.

3   King, *ibid,* 11.

4   Milligan, *ibid,* 27.

5   Milligan, *ibid,* 28.

The Author

This is perhaps the biggest question about the book since the author's name is not found in the book. Origen is reported to have said, "Who wrote the epistle, God only knows."[6] However, it doesn't seem that the letter was completely anonymous to the recipients (Heb. 13:19).

Suggested authors. Some of those who have been suggested as possible authors of the book of Hebrews are: Paul, Clement of Rome, Apollos, Aquila, Barnabas, Luke, Mark, Silas, and Philip the evangelist. The traditional view is that it is the apostle Paul.

Evidence that Paul was the author. The following leads us to believe that Paul was probably the author of the book.

1. **The early writers ("Church Fathers") attribute the book to Paul**. These writers include, Clement of Alexandria (ca 187), Origen (ca 185), Pantaenus (ca 185), Eusebius (ca 264-320), Tertullian (ca 190-200), and Jermone (ca 392).[7] "Save for the occasional voice against it, Hebrews was generally taken as Pauline until the Reformation, when Erasmus vigorously fought for a change in this opinion."[8]

2. **The fact that it was anonymous fits Paul's circumstance**. The author had some valid reason for withholding his name. The early writers mentioned above alleged that Paul withheld his name lest its appearance keep some Jewish brethren from reading it. The strong prejudice against Paul would well fit this situation.

3. **The writer had close association with Timothy (Heb. 13:23).** While others could have such a close relationship, we know Paul did (cf. 1 Tim. 1:2; 2 Tim. 1:2; 2:1).

4. **The writer had been in chains (Heb. 10:34; 13:18-19, 23).** Obviously, Paul had been in prison in Rome (Acts 28).

5. **The writer was (or at least had been) in Italy (Heb. 13:24).** Paul was there in two imprisonments.

6. **There are terms and phrases used in the book that are very similar to Paul's.**[9]

---

6   Gareth L. Reese, *Hebrews*, xxi. Reese argues that Origen was talking about who the amanuensis (one who writes what another dictates) was.
7   For more details see Milligan, *ibid.*, 6-12.
8   King, *ibid.*, 22.
9   This list is compiled from King, *ibid.*, 28-29 and David McClister, *A Commentary on Hebrews*, 8.

Subject	Hebrews	Paul's Writings/ Preaching
Milk and solid food	Heb. 5:13-14	1 Cor. 3:2
Quotes Hab. 2:4	Heb. 10:38	Rom. 1:17; Gal. 3:11
Quotes Psa. 2:7	Heb. 1:5	Acts 13:33
Signs and wonders	Heb. 2:4	Rom. 15:19; 2 Cor. 12:12
World consist by Christ	Heb. 2:10	Rom. 11:36; Col. 1:16
Descendants of Abraham	Heb. 2:16	Gal. 3:29; Rom. 4:16
Word compared to sword	Heb. 4:12	Eph. 6:17
If God permits	Heb. 6:3	1 Cor. 16:7
Confidence by blood	Heb. 10:19	Rom 5:2; Eph. 2:18

7. The writer was not one of the twelve (Heb. 2:3). The statement, "...which at the first began to be spoken by the Lord, and was confirmed to us by those who heard Him" does not exclude an apostle. It just excludes the original twelve. That would obviously fit the apostle Paul.

Arguments that Paul was not the writer. Our limited space will not permit us to look at all the objections to Paul's authorship of Hebrews. However, we will consider three such contentions.

1. The style of Hebrews is different from the style of Paul's writings. Robert Milligan perceived this to be the strongest argument against a Pauline authorship.[10] This is not completely true. We have already noticed above some phrases similar to Paul's others writings. We shall notice later in this introduction that the writer has five major sections where a warning or exhortation follows a doctrinal section. That is very much in the style of Paul. However, we do have to admit that Hebrews is different from other writings by the apostle. Yet, that doesn't mean that the author is different. Deuteronomy is different from Genesis. But they have the same writer. A different audience and different circumstance warrants a different style.

2. The author was dependent upon others to learn the revelation (Heb. 2:3); whereas Paul was independent in learning the revelation (Gal. 1:11-24). "The author's use of the second person plural 'us' in the passage may only be employed in order to more fully identify with the Jewish Christian audience to which he is directing his remarks."[11] The writer of Hebrews does the same in Hebrews 6:1 when he says those who have failed to grow need to go on to perfection. Surely, he was not including himself in the delinquent.

3. Paul was an apostle to the Gentiles, but this letter is to the Hebrews. Paul's work was not confined to the Gentiles (Acts 9:15). He preached to Jews and Gentiles (Acts 13).

Arthur Pink cited 2 Peter 3:15 (where Peter said Paul wrote some things hard to be understood) and concluded, "If the Epistle to the Hebrews be not *that* writing, where is it?"[12]

---

10 *ibid.*, 13.
11 King, *ibid.*, 23.
12 Arthur Pink, *Exposition of Hebrews*, 18.

The Recipients

This is perhaps the second biggest question about the book of Hebrews. "On this question, the critics are still much divided."[13] However, it is agreed that the letter was written to Jewish brethren, but *where* is the question.

Various suggestions. Some think these Jewish Christians were in Italy (based upon Hebrews 13:24). Other suggestions include Greece, Galatia, Spain, and Egypt. The most common thought is that the letter was sent to Jews living in Palestine.

Evidence that this letter was intended for Jewish Christians in Palestine. The following evidence leads us to believe that the recipients lived in Palestine.

1. **It harmonizes with the title "to Hebrews."** "...it follows that the Epistle was, as is generally supposed, addressed to the Jewish Christians in Palestine. For they were the only body of Christians in that age who spoke the Hebrew language (or rather the Aramaic, which was a corruption of the Hebrew)."[14]

2. **Those addressed were familiar with the Mosaic economy.** The mention of the law, the priest, the tabernacle and the sacrifices is without explanation. Those in Palestine (particularly Jerusalem) would have been most familiar with all the rites and ceremonies of the Old Testament system.

3. **The "Church Fathers" suggested Palestine as the destination.** "So far as they have expressed any opinion on the subject, it is to the effect, that the Epistle was addressed to the Jewish Believers in Palestine."[15]

4. **There is no reference to the Jew-Gentile controversy that was prevalent outside of Palestine.**

5. **The church must have been made up entirely of Jews.** There is no hint of a Gentile or Gentiles concerns in the epistle. This would fit well in Palestine.[16]

6. **Those to whom the letter was written had learned the gospel from the immediate disciples of Christ (Heb. 2:3-4).**

7. **The danger of a relapse into Judaism would have been greater in Palestine (cf. Heb. 6:6; 10:29).** The whole line of argumentation throughout the book shows the danger of returning to Judaism.

8. **There was an immediate crisis looming (3:13; 10:25, 37; 12:27).** The destruction of Jerusalem would certainly make Palestine a candidate for consideration.

---

13   Milligan, *ibid.*, 26.
14   Milligan, *ibid.*, 28.
15   Milligan, *ibid.*, 28.
16   *ibid.*, 15.

More specifically, the church at Jerusalem seems to be indicated. If that be the case, this is not a general epistle as some have supposed. The following sections seem to fit the church at Jerusalem; or at least a particular congregation.

1. **Hebrews 10:32-24**. The conflict shortly after they became Christians would fit well with the situation at Jerusalem (Acts 2, 4, 5).

2. **Hebrews 13:12-14**. The references to the gate and the city would have greater meaning to those in Jerusalem.

3. **Hebrews 13:19, 23**. The fact that Paul plans to see them soon would indicate that he is writing to one congregation.

4. **Hebrews 12:4-8**. They had suffered persecution. Saints in Jerusalem had so suffered (Acts 4, 5).

5. **Hebrews 5:12-14**. They were not new converts. Some time has passed since their becoming Christians.

6. **Hebrews 13:19**. The recipients know the author.

7. **Hebrews 13:23**. The recipients know Timothy.

8. **Hebrews 13:7, 17**. Those to whom the letter was intended had elders.

9. **Hebrews 13:24**. Author Pink argues from this verse that the congregation was of considerable size.[17]

Our conclusion is that the letter was sent to Jewish Christians in Palestine, most likely the church at Jerusalem. "The fact that no church ever laid claim to this Epistle is something that is easily understandable on the ground that after Jerusalem was destroyed no church existed in that location."[18]

To be fair, there are objections to the Palestine (Jerusalem) destination of the letter that must be considered.[19] We will not take the space to address those here. They are not convincing enough to rule out the Jerusalem church as the recipient.

The Place of Writing

The writer mentions that those of Italy send greetings (Heb. 13:24). This would indicate that he was in Italy at the time of the writing. Paul was in Rome for two imprisonments.

---

17   Pink, *ibid.*, 11.
18   King, *ibid.*, 16.
19   See King, *ibid.*, 16 and McClister, *ibid.*, 38-39.

The Date of Writing

The letter was written after 33 A.D. It has been some time since Pentecost (Heb. 5:12). When the writer looks back to former days when they were first obedient (Heb. 10:32-33), he reveals to us that it has been a number of years since Pentecost.

The letter was written before 70 A.D. when Jerusalem was destroyed. The temple was still standing (Heb. 7:8; 9:6-10; 13:10). The priests were still offering sacrifices (Heb. 8:4; 10:11-14). The destruction of Jerusalem was near (10:24-25, 37).

It is probable that Paul is at liberty (Heb. 13:23). He was released from his imprisonment in Rome in 63 A.D.

With that information, we conclude that the letter was written sometime between 63 A.D. and 66 A.D. The later part of that period (65-66 A. D.), would better fit the looming crisis (Heb. 10:24-25, 37; 12:27).

The Purpose and the Message

The purpose is to persuade the Hebrew brethren to persevere to the end (just as they had begun) and not fall back into Judaism. The writer calls his letter a "word of exhortation" (Heb. 13:22). He writes to encourage his readers to remain faithful to Christ.

The problem was severe persecution and discouragement. Pressure was on from Jewish leaders who used any tactic they could.

1. **Persecution**. They had endured persecution in the past, and now they face a circumstance where they need endurance (Heb. 10:32-36). They are dealing with what the writer calls "the chastening of the Lord" (Heb. 12:1-11). The chastening is persecution, for it is peculiar to the sons of God (v. 6).

   > The scribes and rulers exercised all their powers of logic, rhetoric, and sophistry, against the disciples of the despised Nazarene, as they were wont to call our Immanuel; and when the force of argument was unavailing, they had recourse to persecution. Some of them they killed; some, they put into prison; and others, they despoiled of their goods: - and all this they did with the view of putting a stop to the progress of Christianity, and inducing all to follow Moses their leader.[20]

2. **Discouraged**. The treatment they received caused the Jewish Christians to be greatly discouraged. The author pictures them with hands hanging down and knees getting feeble (Heb. 12:12-13). "Hebrews presents us with a picture of Jewish Christians who were confused in their faith, weary of persecution and alienation, and were leaning toward quitting Christianity to find relief from their oppression. Hebrews was written to inform their faith more perfectly and to encourage and warn them not to quit following Christ."[21]

---

20 Milligan, *ibid.*, 32

21 McClister, *ibid.*, 31.

Hebrews 1

Lesson 1
Christ Is Superior To Prophets And Angels

Outline

I. Christ is Superior to Prophets (vv. 1-3)

    A. *In time past God spoke by prophets* (v. 1)

    B. *Now God speaks by his Son* (vv. 2-3)
       1. Who is heir of all things (v. 2)
       2. Through whom he made the worlds (v. 2)
       3. Is the brightness of his glory (v. 3)
       4. Express image of his person (v. 3)
       5. Upholds all things by the word of his power (v. 3)
       6. Purged our sins by himself (v. 3)
       7. Sat down at right hand of God (v. 3)

II. Christ is Superior to Angels (vv. 4-14)

    A. *Has a more excellent name* (vv. 4-5)

    B. *Angels worship him* (v. 6)

    C. *Christ is king—angels are just ministers* (vv. 7-9)
       1. Angels are ministers (v. 7)
       2. God called him "God" and gave him a kingdom (vv. 8-9)
       3. Anointed of God (v. 9)

    D. *Christ is the unchanging creator* (vv. 10-12)
       1. He created the world (v. 10)
       2. Heavens, earth and works will perish (vv. 11-12)
       3. The Son remains (vv. 11-12)

    E. *Christ is Lord—angels were ministering spirits* (vv. 13-14)

Key Verse that Summarizes the Chapter

Hebrews 1:4
Having become so much better than the angels, as He has by inheritance obtained a more excellent name than they.

In this chapter we shall see Christ is superior to prophets and Angels. The writer launches immediately into his subject without any introduction or personal remarks. His first sentence says that God speaks to us by his Son (v. 2). The rest of the book develops that point.

Christ is Superior to Prophets (vv. 1-3)

To the Jew, the prophets were held in high esteem. Thus, if Christ is better than the prophets, he is the one to whom we must give heed.

In time past God spoke by prophets (v. 1). A prophet is one who is a spokesman for another (Exo. 4:16; 7:1; John 4:19). Thus, prophets of God declared his message to the fathers (the Hebrew's ancestors) in ancient times.[1] The message was given at "various times" (in many parts, fragmentary). The revelation of his will was not given all at once. "One prophet has one; another has another element of the truth to proclaim."[2]

God revealed his will in "various ways" (in many ways). At times God used visions and dreams (Num. 12:6), face to face communication (Num. 12:8), and even a donkey (Num. 22:25-31).[3]

This first verse argues for the comparative imperfection of the Old Testament for it was incomplete.

Now God speaks by his Son (vv. 2-3). The "last days" refer to the last dispensation. We are now living in the last days (Acts 2:17; 2 Tim. 3:1; Heb. 1:2; 2 Pet. 3:3).[4] Now God's spokesman is more than a prophet, he is God's only Son. This affirms two things: (1) he is deity (cf. John 5:17-18), and (2) he is God's final spokesman. Being God's Son, he is superior to prophets. The author list seven things that are true of the Son that are not true of any prophet.

1. **He is heir of all things (v. 2).** Because he is God's Son, he is heir. This "is most likely a title of dignity, and shows that Jesus has the supreme place in all the mighty universe."[5] He has the nations as an inheritance (Psa. 2:8). He has all authority (Matt. 28:18). When he was raised and ascended he had all power and dominion (Eph. 1:20-22; Acts 2:36).

2. **He is the one through whom he made the worlds (v. 2).** He is the agent through whom God created the universe (John 1:2-3, 10; Col. 1:15-16; 1 Cor. 8:6; Heb. 11:3).

---

1   From the time of the call of Abraham to Malachi.
2   M. R. Vincent, *Vincent's Word Studies of the New Testament*, Electronic Database. Copyright (c) 1997 by Biblesoft.
3   Vincent argues, "This refers to the difference of the various revelations in contents and form. Not the different ways in which God imparted his revelations to the prophets, but the different ways in which he spoke by the prophets to the fathers: in one way through Moses, in another through Elijah, in others through Isaiah, Ezekiel, etc." (*ibid.*).
4   The last days do not refer to a time immediately before the end of time. Peter declared that he was living in the last days (Acts 2:16-17).
5   Gareth L. Reese, *Hebrews*, 3.

3. He is the brightness of his glory (v. 3). He is the radiance (NASV, NIV) of the glory of God. As the radiance of the sun is to the sun, so Christ is to the Father. All the glory of the sun is seen in its brightness. So the glory of God is seen in Christ (cf. John 14:7-9). "He reflects the glory of God" (RSV).

4. He is the express image of his Person (v 3). "Person" refers to God's essential being. The Son of God is "the exact representation of his being" (NIV, "nature" NASV) or "the very image of his substance" (ASV). The principle here is like that of a rubber stamp and the image that it makes. Nothing is more like the original stamp than the image that it makes on the paper. The RSV renders this, "bears the very stamp of his nature." No one (not even the prophets) could more perfectly represent the Father than the Son.

5. He upholds all things by the word of his power (v. 3). Not only was the Son involved in creating the world, but he upholds (sustains, maintains) the world by his word. Paul, said, "in Him all things consist" (Col. 1:17).

6. He purged our sins by himself (v. 3). "He made purification of sins" (ASV). He purified us from sin by himself. No prophet could do that.

7. He sat down at the right hand of God (v. 3). To sit at one's right hand is a position of highest honor and authority (1 Kings 2:19; Psa. 45:9; 80:17; Matt. 20:20-23; 26:64). Christ is sitting at the right hand of God (Acts 2:33; Eph. 1:20). Furthermore, this phrase emphasizes the finality of his redemptive work. His work is completed, and thus he sits down at the right hand of God.[6]

None of these seven things are true of any prophet!

Christ is Superior to Angels (vv. 4-14)

Here the author introduces his use of the word "better"[7]. Christ is so much better than angels. Why are angels introduced here? The writer shows that Christ is not only superior to prophets, but to angels as well. Angels were viewed as the most exalted beings (outside of God). If Christ is better than angels, he then is better than prophets, Moses, Joshua, Aaron, etc. It is possible that "this Hebrew congregation in its desire to safeguard strict Jewish monotheism may have been tempted to assign Jesus a place in the angelic order."[8] The author lists five things that are true of the Son that are not true of angels.

He has a more excellent name (vv. 4-5). His excellent name is Son (evidence by the supporting quote from Psalm 2:7). No angel was ever called the Son of God. To make his point, the author quotes Psalm 2:7[9] and 2 Samuel 7:14[10] and asks "to which of the angels did He ever say" these things?

---

6   In contrast, under the Mosaic system, the priest stands daily offering sacrifices indicating that their work is never completed (Heb. 10:11).

7   The term "better" is used 13 times: 1:4; 6:9; 7:7, 19, 22; 8:6 (twice); 9:23; 10:34; 11:16, 35, 40; 12:24).

8   Daniel H. King, Sr, *The Book of Hebrews*, Truth Commentaries, 61.

9   The same passage was quoted in Paul's sermon in Acts 13:33-34 where he applied it to the resurrection of Christ.

10 This passage obviously referred to Solomon. Milligan argues that it has a double reference. King argues that it has an indirect reference to the descendants of Solomon which includes the Christ.

Angels worship him (v. 6). The word "again" does not suggest that the firstborn is being brought again into the world (as worded in NKJV, ASV). Rather, it is used to introduce another reference from the Old Testament (as worded in KJV, ESV, RSV, NIV).[11]

What does bringing the "firstborn" into the world mean? "The meaning of the phrase, 'when he bringeth in,' therefore, I take to be, when he introduces him to people; when he makes him known to the world—to wit, by the declaration which he proceeds immediately to quote. 'The first-begotten.' Christ is called the 'first-begotten,' with reference to his resurrection from the dead, in Rev. 1, 5, and Col 1:18. It is probable here, however, that the word is used, like the word 'first-born,' or 'first-begotten' among the Hebrews, by way of eminence."[12]

Where is the quotation that says, "Let all the angels of God worship him?" Some think it is Psalm 97:7, but the text doesn't read exactly like that. It is more probable that it is a quotation from Deuteronomy 32:43 where the Septuagint (LXX) says, "Rejoice ye heavens with him; and let all the angels of God worship him. Let the nations rejoice with his people, and let all the sons of God be strong in him, for he has avenged the blood of his sons."[13] While there are some difficulties with the verse, the point is that angels worship him. Thus, he is superior to angels.

Christ is king—angels are just ministers (vv. 7-9). Here use is made of two Psalms to contrast the Son as God and King to the angels as mere servants.

1. **Angels are ministers (v. 7)**. The author quotes Psalm 104:4 where angels were called spirits (winds ASV), ministers and flames of fire. The point is that angels serve as God's ministers at his beck and call. "The passage 'might' be translated, 'Who maketh his angels winds, and his ministers a flame of fire;' that is, 'who makes his angels like the winds, or as swift as the winds, and his ministers as rapid, as terrible, and as resistless as the lightning.'"[14] Thus, angels are instruments that God uses to carry out his purpose just as wind and flames of fire.

2. **God called him "God" and gave him a kingdom (vv. 8-9)**. The wording of Psalm 45:6-7 is applied to the Son. God the Father called the Son "God." This affirms his deity. The Son was given a throne and kingdom established on righteousness.

3. **Anointed of God (v. 9)**. The Father anointed the Son with the oil of gladness. The anointing here "seems to have reference to his glorification in heaven."[15] This anointing was more or above his companions (the angels). Thus, he is superior.

Christ is the unchanging creator (vv. 10-12). The point here is that, unlike angels, Christ is the creator of the world, and thus continues while the creation wears out and will perish. Psalm 102:25-27 is quoted to make this point.

---

11   The author used the word "again" in similar fashion in 2:13; 10:30.
12   Albert Barnes, *Barnes' Notes*, Electronic Database. Copyright (c) 1997 by Biblesoft.
13   As quoted by Barnes.
14   Albert Barnes, *ibid.*
15   King, *ibid.*, 71.

1. **He created the world (v. 10).** Here the Father refers to the Son as Lord and declares that he created the heavens and the earth.

2. **Heavens, earth and the works will perish (vv. 11-12).** The creation will perish (v.11), grow old (v. 11), be folded up (v. 12) and be changed (v. 12). The material universe is wearing out[16] (like a garment does) and will eventually be destroyed (2 Pet. 3:10).

3. **The Son remains (vv. 11-12).** In contrast, the Son remains (v. 11), his years will not fail (v. 12). He is eternal.

Christ is Lord—angels are ministering spirits (vv. 13-14). The quotation here is from Psalm 110:1. Christ is told by the Father to sit at his right hand (be Lord and ruler) until his enemies are a footstool.[17] God never instructed an angel to sit at his right hand. In contrast, the angels are ministering spirits whom God uses to minister to his people.[18] The point is that Christ is Lord (sitting at God's right hand) while angels are mere servants.

None of these five things are true of any angel!

Use of the Old Testament in this Chapter	
Verse in Chapter 1	Old Testament Reference
v. 5	Psalm 2:7
v. 5	2 Sam. 7:14
v. 6	Deut. 32:43 (LXX)
v. 7	Psalm 104:4
v. 8	Psalm 45:6-7
vv. 10-12	Psalm 102:25-27
v. 13	Psalm 110:1

---

16 These verses affirm that the world is wearing out and deteriorating. This agrees with the Second Law of Thermodynamics. Evolution must have the world constantly building itself up.

17 This refers to a conqueror putting his feet on the neck of his defeated enemy (Josh. 10:22-25).

18 This verse tells us more about what angels *are* than what they *do*. Angels are active today (ministering to Christians). However, exactly what they do and how, we don't know.

Questions

1. Why is it important for the Hebrew writer to show Christ is so much better than prophets and angels?

2. What is meant by God speaking in "various times" and in "various ways"?

3. When are the last days and how do we know?

4. What does it mean that Christ is the brightness of the glory of God?

5. What does it mean that Christ is the image of the person of God?

6. What is meant by Christ upholding all things by the word of his power?

7. What five points are made that show Christ is superior to angels?

8. What evidence does this chapter give that Jesus is deity?

9. Why would the writer need to quote from so many Old Testament passages?

10. What do angels do for Christians today?

Hebrews 2

Lesson 2
Giving Heed And The Humanity Of Christ

Outline

I. Give Heed to the Things Heard (vv. 1-4)

    A. *Lest we drift away* (v. 1)

    B. *Cannot escape if we neglect* (vv. 2-4)
        1. Since disobedience to the Old Covenant was punished (v. 2)
        2. Cannot escape if we disobey the new (vv. 3-4)
            a. First spoken by the Lord (v. 3a)
            b. Was confirmed by signs of the apostles (vv. 3b-4)

II. Christ's Superiority to Angels is Seen Even in His Humanity (vv. 5-18)

    A. *Man's dominion over the world was lost* (vv. 5-8)
        1. Dominion not given to angels (v. 5)
        2. Dominion was given to man (vv. 6-8a)
        3. Dominion was lost (v. 8b)

    B. *Christ became flesh to restore man* (vv. 9-18)
        1. To die to save man (vv. 9-10)
        2. To be one with those sanctified (vv. 11-13)
        3. To destroy the devil and his work (vv. 14-16)
        4. To be a merciful High Priest (vv. 17-18)

Key Verses that Summarize the Chapter

Hebrews 2:1
Therefore we must give the more earnest heed to the things we have heard, lest we drift away.

Hebrews 2:9
But we see Jesus, who was made a little lower than the angels, for the suffering of death crowned with glory and honor, that He, by the grace of God, might taste death for everyone.

This chapter begins with the first of the five warning or admonition sections (vv. 1-4).[1] It is followed by a continuation of the discussion of Christ being superior to angels (vv. 5-18).

Give Heed to the Things Heard (vv. 1-4)

The point here is that since God speaks to us by His Son (1:2), who is superior to prophets and angels, we must give earnest heed[2] to the things we have heard—the gospel (v. 1). To give heed would involve listening and obeying.

Lest we drift away (v. 1). "Our author represents us all as on a stream, the natural tendency of which is to carry us downward to ruin."[3] If we don't give heed, we drift. The KJV uses the word "slip" with a footnote rendering, "run out as leaking vessels."[4] Each of these translations suggest a slow or gradual process to apostasy.

Cannot escape if we neglect (vv. 2-4). A second reason we must give heed is that we cannot escape punishment if we don't.

1. **Since disobedience to the Old Covenant was punished (v. 2).** The word spoken by angels is a reference to the Old Testament. Angels played some part in the giving of Law of Moses (Deut. 33:2; Psa. 68:17; Acts 7:53; Gal. 3:19). What that role was, we do not know.

   That law was "steadfast"[5] or firm. It demanded obedience. Every transgression (going beyond) and disobedience (failure to comply) received just punishment.

2. **Cannot escape if we disobey the new (vv. 2-4).** The writer reasons from the lesser to the greater. If the principle seen above is true of the Old Covenant, how much more is it true of the new? "Neglect" is put in contrast to giving heed (v. 1). To stand in danger of condemnation we do not have to set ourselves in opposition to the will of God. Such a danger comes from mere neglect.

The salvation is called "great" in that it offers full and complete pardon that was not possible through the Old Testament (Heb. 8:12). The message of this great salvation was first spoken by the Lord (v. 3a) during his personal ministry.[6] Then it was preached by the apostles and was confirmed (proven to be true) by the miracles they performed (cf. Mark 16:17-20). These are called "signs" because they give proof, and "wonders" because they are supernatural.[7]

---

1 See the Introduction for a list of all five sections.
2 The ESV and NASV translate this "pay much closer attention".
3 Robert Milligan, *Vol. IX – Epistle to the Hebrews,* New Testament Commentary, 76.
4 A slow drip can lose more liquid (over time) than a major leak (which would receive prompt attention).
5 "Valid" (RSV).
6 Note the contrast between the law "spoken through angels" and the great salvation "spoken by the Lord."
7 From this text we learn that the word *has been* confirmed by miracles. No further confirmation or proof is needed today.

Christ's Superiority to Angels is Seen Even in His Humanity (vv. 5-18)

This section (particularly verses 5-8) is difficult. This is seen when seeking to understand what the "world to come" is (v. 5), whether Psalm 8 is talking about man or Christ, and what is not yet under him (v. 8a). This is thorny in that each of the possible positions has some difficulty, including the one presented here. However, let us not lose sight of the overall picture in these verses, which all agree to be that the Son became flesh (to die for man) and in doing so he proved that he was superior to angels.

Man's dominion over the world was lost (vv. 5-8). The point here is that God intended for man to have the honor and glory of dominion over His creation (cf. Gen. 1:28). However that was never fully realized after the fall of man. However, the glory and honor that God intended for man is accomplished through Christ.

1. **Dominion not given to angels (v. 5).** The subjection of the world was not given to angels, but was given to man as seen in verses 6-8. The glory and honor of dominion was not given to angels, but to man. Since that glory is realized through Christ, the "world to come" may refer to the time of the Messiah[8] of which the writer was speaking (1:1-14; 2:1-4).

2. **Dominion was given to man (vv. 6-8a).** The writer quotes from Psalm 8:4-6 wherein the Psalmist shows how God was mindful of man and crowned him with glory by setting him over the works of God's hands. He thus put all things under man (vv. 7-8a).

3. **Dominion was lost (v. 8b).** "But now we do not yet see all things put under him" tells us that because of sin, that intended glory, honor and dominion of man (God's original intent) was never fully realized. "Indeed man is not in complete control of his environment; because of sin, we are subject to disease and death from many forces that can overcome us. We have lost the glory and honor that God originally planned for us."[9]

Christ became flesh to restore man (vv. 9-18). The honor that was held by man (before the fall) will be regained in Christ. This further shows that Christ is superior to angels *even* in his humanity. Perhaps some would question how he could be superior to angels while being made lower than angels (a reference to humanity). If in his death he brings sons to glory (v.10), then he is superior to angels.

1. **To die to save man (vv. 9-10).** "But we see Jesus" shows a contrast. Man does not fully enjoy the dominion of which the Psalmist speaks, but we see the fulfillment of it in Jesus. He was made lower than angels[10] (became flesh) that he should die and save man. In doing so the author is saying "he was crowned with glory and honor, and that he thus fulfilled all that David (Ps 8) had said of the dignity and honor of man."[11] His suffering made him "perfect" (completely fitted) to be our savior. Only through his suffering is salvation possible.

---

8   It is "to come" from the vantage point of the Old Testament and its prophecies.
9   Johnny Stringer, *Hebrews*, Bible Text Books, 5.
10   The NASV: "made for a little while lower than angels" (also RSV, ESV).
11   Albert Barnes, *Barnes' Notes*, Electronic Database. Copyright (c) 1997 by Biblesoft.

2. To be one with those sanctified (vv. 11-13). By becoming flesh he becomes one with those who are sanctified. That is, being of one Father, he shares brotherhood with them. The Old Testament quotation in verse 12 is from Psalm 22:22. This messianic Psalm has the savior calling the saved his brethren. Two additional quotations are given in verse 13. The first of those is from 2 Samuel 22:3 (and Psalm 18:2).[12] Here the picture is of Jesus in his flesh putting his trust in the Father (as the children of God do), thus making him one with them. The last quotation is from Isaiah 8:18.[13] As in the previous reference, the Christ is identified with the children of God (making them brethren), thus they are one.

3. To destroy the devil and his work (vv. 14-16). Jesus became flesh that he might destroy the devil (render him powerless by making it possible for man to escape his snares). By destroying the devil he delivers those who were held captive by him. While they were in bondage and without hope, they had every reason to fear death (v. 15). The aid his death provides was not for angels, but for man (v. 16).

4. To be a merciful High Priest (vv. 17-18). By becoming flesh, Christ becomes a merciful High Priest for he knows the suffering and temptation that man faces. Chapter one shows he is deity. Chapter two shows he was human. Thus, he is the perfect High Priest.

Even in his humanity and suffering he is superior to angels.

Use of the Old Testament in this Chapter	
Verse in Chapter 2	Old Testament Reference
vv. 6-8	Psalm 8:4-6
v. 12	Psalm 22:22
v. 13	2 Samuel 22:3 / Psalm 18:2
v. 13	Isaiah 8:18

---

12   The Psalm is found in both passages.
13   Portions of this chapter are quoted in the NT and applied to Christ (Matt. 21:44; Rom. 9:33; 1 Pet. 2:7-8).

Questions

1. What is the warning or admonition given in 2:1-4?

2. What does this warning say about how apostasy comes? Why is this so dangerous?

3. What two reasons are given for giving heed to the things heard?

4. What does the use of the word "neglect" in this text suggest to us?

5. How do verse 3-4 show that miracles are not needed today?

6. Give a short summary of the point of verses 5-18.

7. How does the humanity of Jesus show he is superior to angels?

8. What dominion did God intend for man to have according to Psalm 8?

9. In what way is Christ and those who are sanctified one (vv. 11-13)?

10. How does becoming flesh make Jesus the perfect High Priest?

Hebrews 3

Lesson 3
Christ Is Superior To Moses And Don't Harden Your Heart

Outline

I. **Christ is Superior to Moses** (vv. 1-6)

    A. *Christ is the faithful Apostle and High Priest in his house* (vv. 1-2)

    B. *Christ is the builder of his house* (vv. 3-4)

    C. *Christ is the Son over his house* (vv. 5-6)

II. **Don't Harden Your Heart** (vv. 7-19)

    A. Warning from the example of Israel (vv. 7-11)
       1. They hardened their heart (vv. 7-9)
       2. They did not enter into rest (vv. 10-11)

    B. *Beware lest you depart in unbelief* (vv. 12-15)
       1. Beware (v. 12)
       2. Exhort one another (v. 13)
       3. Hold the beginning of our confidence (v. 14)
       4. Hear his voice (v. 15)

    C. *Those of Israel who rebelled* (vv. 16-19)
       1. All who came out of Egypt (v. 16)
       2. Did not enter into rest (vv. 18-19)
       3. Why? (vv. 17-19)
          a. Sinned (v. 17)
          b. Did not obey (v. 18)
          c. Unbelief (v. 19)

Key Verses that Summarize the Chapter

Hebrews 2:1
For this One has been counted worthy of more glory than Moses, inasmuch as He who built the house has more honor than the house.

Hebrews 2:9
Do not harden your hearts as in the rebellion, in the day of trial in the wilderness.

Having established that Christ is superior to prophets and angels, the author now proceeds to show that Christ is superior to Moses. Then he turns to the second of the five warning sections.[1]

Christ is Superior to Moses (vv. 1-6)

Moses was one of the most significant figures in the mind of a Jew; perhaps second to Abraham. Any appeal to turn back to Judaism would be an appeal to follow Moses. Hence the need to demonstrate that Christ is far above Moses.

Here the Hebrew Christians are addressed as "partakers of the heavenly calling." Their call to salvation was from heaven and pertained to going to heaven. "The older religion was an earthly calling with an earthly inheritance. Christianity is a spiritual religion involving a heavenly calling with a spiritual and heavenly inheritance as its ultimate object."[2]

Christ is the faithful Apostle and High Priest in his house (vv. 1-2). The reader is urged to consider[3] Jesus, the Apostle and High Priest. An apostle is one sent forth. Thus, Jesus is called an apostle in that he was sent by God (Gal. 4:4). He is our High Priest as seen in the previous chapter. Being the Apostle and High Priest are not necessarily separate offices. He was sent (thus an Apostle) as the High Priest.

> But the connection seems to demand that; there should be some allusion here to one who sustained a similar rank among the Jews; and it is prob-able that the allusion is to Moses, as having been the great apostle of God to the Jewish people, and that Paul here means to say, that the Lord Jesus, under the new dispensation, filled the place of Moses AND of the high priest under the old, and that the office of "apostle" and "high priest," instead of being now separated, as it was between Moses and Aaron under the old dispensation, was now blended in the Messiah.[4]

The reader is told that Jesus is the Apostle and High Priest of their confession. They had held to and publicly acknowledged who he was. "The full meaning of this confession had obviously been missed by some of these readers, but this is not all that surprising, for it carried with it results which were of a revolutionary nature for the Jewish mind."[5]

Moses is never called an apostle, but he was one in that he was sent by God (Exo. 3:10, 13, 15; 4:28; 5:22; 7:16; Acts 7:35). He was faithful as God's servant (Num. 12:7). The comparison is obvious. Both Moses and Jesus are said to be faithful in God's house.

Christ is the builder of his house (vv. 3-4). Christ is worthy of more glory than Moses just as a builder has more glory and honor than the house. God is the builder of all things (v. 5).[6] This gives us evidence of the deity of Christ. He is the builder (v. 3), but God is said to be the builder (v. 4). Thus, Jesus Christ is God!

---

1   See the Introduction for a list of all five sections.
2   Daniel H. King, Sr, *The Book of Hebrews*, Truth Commentaries, 106.
3   This means "to observe fully" (Strong's). They were to meditate and give careful at-tention to what is said about Jesus and what that means.
4   Albert Barnes, *Barnes' Notes*, Electronic Database. Copyright (c) 1997 by Biblesoft.
5   King, *ibid.*, 107.
6   Perhaps the author is alluding to Psalm 127:1.

Moses was in God's house, but Christ is the builder of God's house[7]. Thus, he is superior.

Christ is the Son over his house (vv. 5-6). Moses was a faithful servant in God's house (Num. 12:7). His service and work served as a testimony pointing to better things. Moses was involved in the preparation, but Christ was the fulfillment. Christ holds the exalted positon of Son over his own house. The people of God are that house of God, but conditioned upon holding fast and remaining firm to the end (v. 6).

Don't Harden Your Heart (vv. 7-19)

Here the author begins the second of the five warning sections of the book that continues through much of the next chapter (4:16). The warning is against hardening the heart and rebelling like Israel of old did under Moses.

Warning from the example of Israel (vv. 7-11). The writer quotes from Psalm 95:7-11 and attributes that to the Holy Spirit.[8] This Psalm pleads for obedience today lest the heart become hardened.[9] To refuse or delay obedience has a hardening effect on the heart.

They hardened their heart (vv. 7-9). This Psalm points to Israel's rebellion in the wilderness when they murmured against Moses and the Lord because they had no water (Exo. 17:1-7). There in the wilderness they put God to the test by constantly complaining and rebelling, although they witnessed God's works for forty years (cf. Num. 14:22).

They did not enter into rest (vv. 10-11). Because they hardened their hearts and didn't obey, God's anger was stirred. They were always going astray.[10] God said, "they have not known my ways" (v. 10).[11] Thus, he swore that they would not enter into their rest in the land of Canaan (Num. 14:21-24).

Daniel King's observation is worth considering: "Since the first case cited appeared at the beginning of the wilderness wanderings and the second appeared at the end, this suggests that the hardening of their hearts was a process that persisted over the entire forty years of their wanderings."[12]

Beware lest you depart in unbelief (vv. 12-15). Here application is made from the Psalm. If the Hebrews did not take heed, they will depart, just like Israel, to the point of unbelief. The warning is that it could happen to "any of you" (v. 12). Thus, there are four things they are told to do:

Beware (v. 12). In view of the ever present danger, each Christian should "take heed" (KJV, "take care" ESV), constantly checking his spiritual condition.

---

7   Christ is the "Founder of all things, including the Jewish Theocracy as well as the Christian Church" (Robert Milligan, *Vol. IX – Epistle to the Hebrews*, New Testament Commentary, 116).

8   Later he quotes the same Psalm and attributes it to David (4:7). This affirms that David wrote by inspiration (cf. 2 Pet. 1:21).

9   Notice each time the term "today" is used in this chapter and the next, it is contrasted to hardening the heart (3:7-8, 13, 15; 4:7).

10 Compare the statement "have put Me to the test now these ten times" (Num. 14:22).

11 Perhaps "have not heeded My voice" is a parallel phrase (Num. 14:22).

12 King, *ibid.*, 113.

Exhort one another (v. 13). "Each reader of this letter to the Hebrews is to be an encourager of his brethren."[13] The fact that they were to do this daily, while it is "today", may point to some urgency due to a looming crisis (i.e. the destruction of Jerusalem in A.D.70).

If we fail to exhort one another the danger is ever increased that some of us will be hardened by the deceitfulness of sin. "If the members of every congregation of disciples, would all watch over one another, not as censors, but as members of the body of Christ, how many errors might be corrected in their incipiency. But as it is, how very different are the results. How many delinquent Christians are allowed to become hardened in sin before even the Elders of the Church call on them and admonish them!"[14]

Hold the beginning of our confidence (v. 14). To be partakers with Christ and not depart, one must hold firm and steadfast to the confidence he had when he obeyed the gospel. This connects with what was professed (confessed) at the time (cf. v. 1).

Hear his voice (v. 15). Since the "end" (v. 14) had not been reached, the reader is admonished to hear the voice of God (who speaks through his Son, 1:1). He again quotes from Psalm 95:7-8 to make his point.

Those of Israel who rebelled (vv. 16-19). The point here is to emphasize how great the danger of falling is by showing how many fell in the wilderness before reaching the promise land. That number was "all who came out of Egypt" (v. 16). While there were exceptions (i.e. Joshua and Caleb), the author is focusing on the greater picture. It wasn't a select few that fell, but the whole group (of these that came out of Egypt). They were not allowed to enter into their rest (vv. 18-19). That number sends a strong warning to us.

The reason for their fall was their sin (v. 17), their disobedience (v. 18), and their unbelief (v. 19; cf. v. 12).

The parallel is clear. The Israelites came out of Egypt and fell before reaching the promise land. The same could happen to the Hebrew and to us. We could easily fall before reaching our land of rest (heaven).

Israel	Bondage of Egypt	Water of Red Sea	Wilderness Wandering (Many fell before they made it...)	Promise Land
Today	Bondage of Sin	Water of Baptism	Now (We too could fall before...)	Heaven – Our Promise Land

Use of the Old Testament in this Chapter	
Verse in Chapter 3	Old Testament Reference
vv. 7-11	Psalm 95:7-11
v. 15	Psalm 95:7-8

---

13 Gareth L. Reese, *Hebrews*, 48.
14 Milligan, *ibid.*, 125.

Questions

1. What arguments are given to show that Christ is superior to Moses?

2. In what sense was Christ an apostle?

3. Was Moses an apostle? If so, how do we know?

4. Is the Hebrew writer trying to diminish Moses in the mind of the Hebrews?

5. What evidence is found in this chapter that Jesus is deity?

6. Summarize the warning (vv. 7-19) in one sentence.

7. What do we learn from the fact that Psalm 95 is attributed to the Holy Spirit?

8. What is to be learned from the quotation of Psalm 95?

9. What does verse 12 tell us about how great the danger of apostasy is?

10. What point is to be learned from how many fell in the wilderness (v. 16)?

Hebrews 4

Lesson 4
Warning Not To Fail And Hold Fast

Outline

I. **Warning Not to Fail as Israel Did** (vv. 1-13)

    A. *Let us fear lest we come short* (vv. 1-2)
        1. Since a promise remains of entering rest (v 1)
        2. Since the word preached to Israel did not profit them (v. 2)

    B. *There remains a rest to those who believe* (vv. 3-10)
        1. Seen in Psalm 95 (vv. 3, 5)
        2. Seen in the Sabbath rest (vv. 3b-4)
        3. Seen in the fact that Israel did not enter (vv. 6-9)
        4. Seen in the fact that one who enters ceases work (v. 10)

    C. *Let us be diligent lest we fall* (vv. 11-13)
        1. Just like Israel in their disobedience (v. 11)
        2. For God sees all and knows all (vv. 12-13)

II. **Hold Fast Because of Our High Priest** (vv. 14-16)

    A. *Jesus is our High Priest in heaven* (v. 14)

    B. *He knows our needs and problems* (v. 15)

    C. *He gives help in time of need* (v. 16)

Key Verses that Summarizes the Chapter

Hebrews 4:11
Let us therefore be diligent to enter that rest, lest anyone fall according to the same example of disobedience.

Hebrews 4:14
Seeing then that we have a great High Priest who has passed through the heavens, Jesus the Son of God, let us hold fast our confession.

This chapter concludes the warning or admonition that began at 3:7. This is the second of the five warning sections. It would be helpful to take a moment to look back at the first part of this section (3:7-19).

Warning Not to Fail as Israel Did (vv. 1-13)

The point of this section is to learn from Israel's example and not fail to enter as they did.

Let us fear lest we come short (vv. 1-2). Having stated that Israel did not enter because of unbelief (3:19), the writer urges his readers to fear (be watchful, cautious, careful) lest they come short of entering that rest. The fact that so many have fallen should cause us to fear.

Since a promise remains of entering rest (v. 1). In that Israel did not enter their rest, a promise remains to be fulfilled. This point will be developed more in verses 3-10.

Since the word preached did not profit them (v. 2). The gospel (good news of a promised rest) was preached to Israel of old just like the gospel (good news of a promised rest) is preached to us. However, the gospel did not profit them because it was not mixed with faith.[1] For the gospel to be of any profit we must add faith to what we hear.

There remains a rest to those who believe (vv. 3-10). These verses develop the thought introduced at verse 1: a rest remains for those who have believed[2] (v. 3).

Seen in Psalm 95 (vv. 3, 5). In proof of this point, an appeal is made to Psalm 95:11 where we are told that God swore to Israel they would not enter the rest in Canaan. The fact that some were refused rest because of unbelief (disobedience) suggests that some would receive rest if they believed (obeyed).

Seen in the Sabbath rest (vv. 3b- 4). Those who came out of Egypt did not enter rest "although the works were finished from the foundation of the world" (v. 3b). The point is that God finished his work of creation and then rested. Thus, his rest that he offers to man has been available since then. Israel's failure to enter was not because God had not made it available.

Confirming his point just made, the author quotes Genesis 2:2 where it is stated that God rested on the seventh day. The Sabbath rest serves as a type of all the rest that would follow. The fact, that God entered rest suggests that he desires the same for his people.

Seen in the fact that Israel did not enter (vv. 6-9). From what was said in verses 3-5 the conclusion is drawn that there remains a rest that some must enter (v. 6). However, those

---

1   The mixing may have reference to mixing or uniting with those who are believers. "The problem with the majority of people in the exodus generation is that they did not join themselves (they **were not united**), **in faith** to those few who did 'hear' God's word" (David McClister, *A Commentary on Hebrews*, 162).
2   Since "believed" is past tense, it probably is a reference to the point at which they were converted. The point to be learned is that the promise of rest is held out to those who remain faithful, unlike Israel of old.

to whom that promise was first proclaimed (those who came out of Egypt) did not enter that rest because of disobedience (v. 6b).[3]

A question could be raised about those who did enter the Canaan rest under the leadership of Joshua. Did they fulfill the promise of rest so that such hope does not remain? The answer is no because David[4] spoke of "today" heeding the voice of God and entering that rest (Psa. 95:7-8). That was a "long time" after Joshua[5] lead them into the land. If that had fulfilled the promised rest, David would not have spoken of another day to come (v. 8). Thus, the writer concludes, "There remains therefore a rest for the people of God" (v. 9).

Seen in the fact that one who enters ceases work (v. 10). "For" connects this verse to the previous thought: there remains a rest (v. 9). One reason for saying this is that one[6] who enters into rest ceases from his work just like God ceased his work when he rested.

Let us be diligent lest we fall (vv. 11-13). Since a rest remains to those who are faithful, we must be diligent[7] to enter that rest. If we don't, we will fall just like Israel in their disobedience (v. 11). Note the warning is to "anyone" (v. 11). Each of us need to take heed lest we fall (1 Cor. 10:12).

We must be diligent for God sees all and knows all (vv. 12-13). The word of God is living and powerful. Thus, any promise or warning is real! Being sharper than a two edged sword, it can pierce and divide soul and spirit as well as joints and marrow. The word of God can penetrate the innermost part of man and lay bare all that is there. That is explained in the last expression of verse 12. By his word, God discerns the thoughts and intents of man's heart. "God's Word is like a two-edged sword, sharp as a scalpel, discerning every twist and turn of the human mind. That is the essence of the writer's meaning here."[8]

The writer turns from the word to God himself (v. 13) and declares all things are open[9] to the eyes of the one to whom we must give an account.

---

3   The KJV uses the word "unbelief." The NKJV and ASV use the word "disobedience." Compare this verse with Hebrews 3:19 where "unbelief" is used. Disobedience is a form of unbelief.

4   Hebrews 3:7 attributed this quotation to the Holy Spirit. Thus, David spoke by inspiration.

5   The KJV says "Jesus" (v. 8). This is a reference to Joshua (NKJV, ASV). The spelling is the same in Greek. The context also shows this is speaking of Joshua.

6   Some think the one who enters is a reference to Christ (cf. LBP). However the context points to the people of God (v. 9).

7   KJV says "labor." Diligence suggest that we exert every ounce of energy to enter that rest.

8   Daniel H. King, Sr, *The Book of Hebrews*, Truth Commentaries, 139.

9   "The idea at the root seems to be the bending back of the neck, and the last explanation, better than any other, suits the previous figure of the sword. The custom of drawing back the victim's neck for sacrifice is familiar to all Classical students... The victim's throat bared to the sacrificial knife is a powerful figure of the complete exposure of all created intelligence to the eye of him whose word is as a two-edged sword" (M. R. Vincent, *Vincent's Word Studies of the New Testament*, Electronic Database. Copyright (c) 1997 by Biblesoft).

Hold Fast Because of Our High Priest (vv. 14-16)

The reader is urged to hold fast to the confession or profession that has been made (cf. 3:1). This is another way of saying be diligent (v. 11) or be faithful. This is possible because of the High Priest we have.

Jesus is our High Priest in heaven (v. 14). Our High Priest is Jesus, the Son of God (deity). He has ascended into the most holy place, heaven itself. What a contrast to the high priest under the Mosaic economy!

He knows our needs and problems (v. 15). Our High Priest can sympathize with our weakness because he became flesh (chapter 2) and was tempted[10] as we are, yet he did not sin. He understands our trials and struggles.

He gives help in time of need (v. 16). Since we have such an understanding High Priest, we should come boldly before the throne of grace.[11] What an honor that all Christians have access to the very throne of deity (cf. Eph. 2:13). "There is not merely grace on the throne, but the throne is altogether the throne of grace. It is grace which disciplines us by the sharp and piercing Word. It is grace that looks on us when we have denied Him and makes us weep bitterly. Jesus always intercedes: the throne is always a throne of grace. The Lamb is in the midst of the throne. Hence we come boldly."[12] We come boldly ("with confidence" ESV, NASV) because we understand the merciful God we are approaching.

In so doing we find mercy and grace in time of need.[13] As we strive to enter the rest that awaits us (v. 11) there will be problems and struggles along the way. There will be temptation and trials. Approaching God's gracious throne we will find mercy and grace that we need. We cannot make our journey toward heaven without the help of our High Priest. Raymond Brown said, "...prayerlessness is the root of all sin. When we do not give time each day to earnest and believing prayer, we are saying that we can cope with life without divine aid. It is human arrogance at its worst...to be prayerless is to be guilty of the worst form of practical atheism."[14]

Use of the Old Testament in this Chapter	
Verse in Chapter 4	Old Testament Reference
v. 3	Psalm 95:11
v. 4	Genesis 2:2
v. 5	Psalm 95:11
v. 7	Psalm 95:7-8

---

10 Tempted in all points simply means that he was tempted by all avenues of sin: lust of the flesh, lust of the eye and the pride of life (1 John 2:15-17; Matt. 4:1-11).

11 The ASV and ESV have "draw near." The NIV: "approach."

12 Arthur Pink, *Exposition of Hebrews*, 220.

13 A. T. Robertson suggests that "in time of need" gives the idea of "'For well-timed help,' 'for help in the nick of time,' before it is too late" (*Robertson's Word Pictures in the New Testament*, Electronic Database. Copyright (c) 1997 by Biblesoft & Robertson's Word Pictures in the New Testament. Copyright (c) 1985 by Broadman Press).

14 As quoted by King, *ibid.*, 146-147.

Questions

1. In what sense were the Hebrews told to fear and why were they to fear?

2. How was the gospel preached to Israel in the Old Testament (v. 2)?

3. How does Psalm 95 show that a rest remains for the people of God?

4. What does "although the works were finished from the foundation of the world" mean?

5. How does the Sabbath rest show that a rest remains for the people of God?

6. When Joshua led Israel into Canaan, did that fulfill the promise of a rest?

7. What does the word "anyone" (v. 11) tell us?

8. What point is being made by saying the word can pierce and divide soul and spirit as well as joints and marrow?

9. In what way is our High Priest (Jesus) superior to the high priest under the Mosaic economy?

10. How does Jesus being our High Priest relate to the warnings in the rest of the chapter?

Hebrews 5

Lesson 5
Christi Is A Better High Priest

Outline

I. Christ is Qualified as our High Priest (vv. 1-10)

    A. *Qualifications and function of a high priest* (vv. 1-4)
        1. From among men (v. 1)
        2. Functions for man (v. 1)
        3. Offers gifts and sacrifices (v. 1,3)
        4. Is acquainted with infirmities of man (v. 2-3)
        5. Appointed of God (v. 4)

    B. *Christ qualifies for the perfect High Priest* (vv. 5-10)
        1. Appointed of God (vv. 5-6, 10)
            a. Didn't glorify self (v. 5)
            b. God: "after the order of Melchizedek (vv. 6, 10)
        2. Had "days in the flesh" (v. 7)
            a. Thus, from among men
            b. Thus, acquainted with man's infirmities
        3. He suffered death (vv. 8-9)
            a. His sacrifice: himself
            b. Thus, he is perfect High Priest
            c. Offers eternal salvation to all who obey

II. The Hebrew's Lack of Maturity (vv. 11-14)

    A. *Dull of hearing* (v. 11)
        1. Have much to say about the subject (v. 11a)
        2. Thus, hard to explain a difficult subject (v. 11b)

    B. *In need of first principle teaching* (vv. 12-14)
        1. Ought to be teachers, but are not (v. 12a)
        2. In need of milk and not solid food (vv. 12b-14)
            a. Milk – for babes and unskilled (v. 13)
            b. Solid food – for full age and exercised (v. 14)

Key Verse that Summarizes the Chapter

Hebrews 5:6

As He also says in another place: "You are a priest forever According to the order of Melchizedek."

It would be helpful to turn back to the outline of the book found in the Introduction. There you will see that the author made a shift in emphasis beginning at the end of the previous chapter. The focus has been on the superiority of Christ's *person* (1:1 – 4:13). Now the focus is on the superiority of Christ's *work* (4:14 – 10:18).

In this chapter attention is given to the priesthood of Christ. More details will be given in chapters 7.

Christ is Qualified as our High Priest (vv. 1-10)

Christ being our High Priest was introduced twice before we get to this chapter (3:1; 4:14-16). The obvious question, for the Hebrews, would be how could Jesus (from the tribe of Judah) qualify to be High Priest since priests were to come from the tribe of Levi? These ten verses show that he is not only qualified to be High Priest, but is better than those of the lineage of Aaron.

Qualifications and function of a high priest (vv. 1-4). Here are five principles that were true of every high priest from the Aaronic priesthood.

From among men (v. 1). A high priest was taken from among men (Exo. 28:1). Thus, he understand the needs of those whom he serves. If he were taken from among the angelic order, he could not relate to the struggles of man.

Functions for man (v. 1). The high priest is appointed *for* man. His work is for the benefit of man, not God. He functions "in things pertaining to God" (v. 1), that is in that which has to do with man's relationship with God.

Offers gifts and sacrifices (vv. 1, 3). The work of the high priest was to offer gifts (those of the bloodless nature) and sacrifices (blood offerings).

Is acquainted with infirmities of man (vv. 2-3). The high priest would have compassion ("bear gently" ASV) with those who sinned out of ignorance or weakness, because he himself was a sinner.[1] Thus, he offers sacrifice for himself as well as for the people (v. 3).

Appointed of God (v. 4). No man takes the honor of the priesthood on himself. Aaron and his sons didn't arbitrarily assume their positions. Rather, they were appointed by God (Exo. 28:1).

Christ qualifies for the perfect High Priest (vv. 5-10). The author now shows that Christ meets the qualifications.

Appointed of God (vv. 5-6, 10). Christ did not glorify himself by appointing himself to be High Priest (v.5a). Rather, the Father said to him "You are My Son, Today I have begotten You" (Psalm 2:7). This Psalm had reference to the resurrection of Christ (Acts 13:33). Two things we learn from this Psalm. First, Christ is the Son of God (deity). Second, he was declared to be the Son of God when he was raised from the dead.

---

1   Aaron sinned with the golden calf (Exo. 32:1-6), complaining, along with Miriam, against Moses (Num. 12), and was included in the sin of striking the rock (Num. 20:1-13).

What does the fact that he is God's Son and that he was raised from the dead have to do with his priesthood? He is saying that the one who called him his Son, is the same one who called him a priest (vv. 6, 10). Thus, he was appointed of God. Furthermore, the one who is our High Priest is the Son of God. His priesthood began when he was raised from the dead to sit at the right hand of God.[2]

The writer quotes from Psalm 110:4 showing that God called him a priest forever[3] after the order of Melchizedek (vv. 6, 10). Melchizedek was king of Salem and priest of God (Gen. 14:17-24).

How is Christ a high priest like Melchizedek? Melchizedek was a king and priest at the same time (Gen. 14). Christ is king and priest at the same time (Zech. 6:12-13). Melchizedek was without father and mother (Heb. 7:3), which means he didn't come to the office through descent, but by appointment. Likewise Christ didn't become priest by earthly lineage. Both were superior to Aaron.[4] Melchizedek was

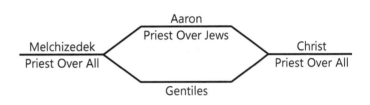

in a one-high-priest priesthood. He was priest over all (long before Aaron was appointed over the Jews). So, Christ is High Priest over all and is the only High Priest. In contrast the Aaronic priesthood was over the Jews only and involved many high priests.

The point here (and in chapter 7) is to prove the claim that Christ is high priest since he is not of the Aaronic priesthood.

Had "days in the flesh" (v. 7). While Christ was in the flesh (thus from among men) he offered up prayers and supplications with vehement cries and tears. This must have reference to his pleading to God in the Garden of Gethsemane (Matt. 26:36-46; Luke 22:39-46). The agony that he displayed shows he was acquainted with man's infirmities.

His plea was to the Father, who was able to save him from death. He was heard because of his godly fear. His prayer was that if possible the cup of suffering would pass, "nevertheless not My will, but Yours, be done" (Luke 22:42). God heard and answered that prayer—that is, his will was done. That prayer showed his deep reverence and devotion to God.[5]

---

2   He would be a king and priest at the same time (Zech. 6:12-13).
3   Forever here means as long as time endures. He is a king and priest at the same time (Zech. 6:12-13). He will be king until the second coming (1 Cor. 15:23-24). Thus, he will cease to be priest at that time as well.
4   This will be developed more in chapter 7 (vv. 4-11).
5   The phrase, "was heard because of His godly fear" is a difficult phrase. Many interpretations have been given. Some think it refers to his fear of death. Others think it refers to his fear of God. Another question has to do with what his request was. Some think he was praying to be raised from the dead, while others think he was praying that the will of God be done. The position presented here makes more sense to this writer.

He suffered death (vv. 8-9). Even though he is God's Son, he was not exempt from obedience (submitting to death). He learned obedience by the experience of suffering. His death made him "perfect" (complete) or fully qualified to serve as High Priest. Through his suffering and death (his sacrifice) he became the author of eternal salvation to all those who obey.[6] Thus, Christ meets all the qualifications to be High Priest. But, more, he is a greater High Priest. He is the Son of God (v. 5, 8). He offers eternal salvation (v. 9).

The Hebrew's Lack of Maturity (vv. 11-14)

This begins the third of five warning sections.[7] This warning about not maturing continues through the end of the next chapter. The discussion of the priesthood of Christ will be taken up again in chapter 7.

Dull of hearing (v. 11). The author had much to say about the subject of the priesthood of Christ being after the order of Melchizedek (v. 11a). But, such a difficult subject is hard to explain because they had become dull of hearing (v. 11b). Their dullness was a mental dullness rather than a literal hearing problem. This is seen in the next three verses.

In need of first principle teaching (vv. 12-14). Enough time had passed[8] that the Hebrews should have become teachers (v. 12). "The Apostle does not mean by this, that the Hebrew brethren should all be teachers in a public and official sense; but simply that they should be able to explain the Gospel to others in their several places and relations, as parents, neighbors, and friends."[9] However, they were not able to do that. In fact, they needed to be taught again the first principles or basic elements of the gospel.[10]

The Hebrews now stand in need of milk and not solid food (vv. 12b-14). Milk is for babes and the unskilled (v. 13). Solid food is for those who are mature or of full age (v. 14). "Whenever adults, who used to be on solid food are reduced to having to eat baby food, it usually signifies they are sick or something is seriously wrong."[11]

The maturity they were lacking comes by having their senses exercised by "reason of use" (v. 14). The idea of use is "habit" (Darby), "constant practice" (ESV), or by "constant use have trained themselves to distinguish good from evil" (NIV). The point is that by use and exercise one's senses are improved. Had the Hebrews exercised and used what knowledge (and faith) they had, it would have grown. Consequently, they would have matured and not be in the danger of falling that they are in now.

Use of the Old Testament in this Chapter	
Verse in Chapter 5	Old Testament Reference
v. 5	Psalm 2:7
v. 6	Psalm 110:4

---

6   The present tense of "obey" suggest continual obedience, which is faithfulness. Thus, a point to which the Hebrews needed to take heed.
7   Look back at the Introduction for a list of the warning sections.
8   Approximately 30 years have passed since the day of Pentecost.
9   Robert Milligan, *Vol. IX – Epistle to the Hebrews*, New Testament Commentary, 166.
10 Not only had they not progressed, but they regressed. They lost or forgot (through neglect) much of what they already knew.
11 Gareth L. Reese, *Hebrews*, 81.

Questions

1. Why does the writer need to address the qualifications of a high priest?

2. What are the five qualifications or functions given in verses 1-4?

3. What does the fact that he is God's Son and that he was raised from the dead have to do with his priesthood?

4. How do we know that Psalm 2:7 is talking about the resurrection of Christ?

5. What does it mean that Christ is priest "according to the order of Melchizedek"?

6. What is the point being made from Psalm 110 about Melchizedek?

7. What point is being made about the prayers, cries, and tears in the days of his flesh (v. 7)?

8. What does "he was heard because of His godly fear" (v. 7) mean?

9. In what sense were the Hebrews dull of hearing?

10. What had created the lack of maturity in the Hebrews?

Hebrews 6

Lesson 6
Encouragement To Go On To Maturity

Outline

I. Encouragement to Go Beyond First Principles (vv. 1-3)

    A. *Must leave the first principles of the doctrine of Christ* (v. 1a)

    B. *Not laying again the foundation* (vv. 1b-2)
        1. Repentance from dead works (v. 1)
        2. Faith toward God (v. 1)
        3. Doctrine of baptisms (v. 2)
        4. Laying on of hands (v.2)
        5. Resurrection of the dead (v. 2)
        6. Eternal judgment (v. 2)

    C. *This we will do* (v. 3)

II. Encouragement Due to the Dangers of Apostasy (vv. 4-8)

    A. *If fall away—impossible to renew* (vv. 4-6)

    B. *End is to be burned* (vv. 7-8)

III. Encouragement Based on Confidence in the Hebrews (vv. 9-12)

    A. *Persuaded better things of the Hebrews* (v. 9)

    B. *You have worked and labored* (v. 10)

    C. *Show the same diligence unto the end* (vv. 11-12)

IV. Encouragement Based on the Promises of God (vv. 13-20)

    A. *God's promises confirmed by an oath* (vv.13-18)
        1. Promise to Abraham was confirmed and received (vv. 13-15)
        2. Assured by two immutable things (vv. 16-18)

    B. *Hope is the anchor of the soul* (vv. 19-20)

```
┌─────────────────────────────────────────────────────────────────────────┐
│ ═══════════ Key Verse that Summarizes the Chapter ═══════════             │
│                                                                           │
│                            Hebrews 6:1                                     │
│ Therefore, leaving the discussion of the elementary principles of Christ, │
│ let us go on to perfection, not laying again the foundation of repentance │
│ from dead works and of faith toward God.                                  │
└─────────────────────────────────────────────────────────────────────────┘
```

This chapter continues the third warning section that began in the previous chapter (5:11-14). There the point was to establish the Hebrews' lack of maturity. Here, the encouragement is given to press on toward the maturity they so needed.

Encouragement to Go Beyond First Principles (vv. 1-3)

The Hebrews not only should know the first principles of the gospel well enough to tell others, but should move beyond those elementary things and grow.

Must leave the first principles of the doctrine of Christ (v. 1a). "Therefore" points back to the Hebrews' immature state (5:11-14). Because of that, they need to go on to maturity.

Students differ over the meaning of the "elementary principles of Christ." Some think it refers to Jewish practices under the Old Testament.[1] It more likely refers to first principles of the gospel for three reasons. 1. The context is dealing with the immaturity of those who have not grown as they should (5:11-14). 2. This is written to Christians, not to those in Judaism who need to leave that and obey the gospel. 3. These are elementary principles "of Christ." The ASV renders this, "leaving the doctrine of the first principles of Christ."[2]

The reader is urged to "leave" the elementary principles. "'Leaving or dismissing' does not imply ceasing to believe in elementary truths or to regard them as important, but leaving them 'as a builder leaves his foundation in erecting his building' (Bruce)."[3] Moving beyond the first principles, one should go on to perfection (maturity).[4]

Not laying again the foundation (vv. 1b-2). As in building a house, the foundation is laid and then the structure is built upon it. The builder doesn't stop at that or keep building the foundation. He moves on. Here the foundation is the same as the first principles. There are six elements listed here that are elementary or foundational. This is not exhaustive.

Repentance from dead works (v.1). All sin produces spiritual death (Jas. 1:15; Rom.6:23). Thus, repenting of sin is repenting of dead works. One of the first things one learns in the gospel is that God demands repentance (Acts 2:38; 17:30-31).

Faith toward God (v. 1). Faith involves full trust and confidence in God. One who turns from sin in repentance, must put his full confidence in God (Heb. 11:6).

---

1   Thus, the point would be that these Hebrew Christians needed to leave the Mosaic system (which was the foundation) and press on to maturity in Christ.
2   Hebrews 5:12 had just mentioned the "first principles of the oracles of God."
3   M. R. Vincent, *Vincent's Word Studies of the New Testament*, Electronic Database. Copyright (c) 1997 by Biblesoft.
4   ESV and footnote of NKJV.

Doctrine of baptisms (v. 2). The plural "baptisms" raises some questions for students of the text. Does this refer to the one baptism (Eph. 4:5)? If not, how were there baptisms under the New Testament? In the first century there was the baptism of the Holy Spirit (Acts 1:5-8) as well as water baptism for the remission of sins (Mark 16:16; Acts 2:38). The difference in the two and which one would last (Eph. 4:5) would be part of the basics of the gospel. Also, in the years immediately following John's baptism people had to be taught the difference in the two baptisms (Acts 19:1-5).

Laying on of hands (v. 2). This probably has reference to how spiritual gifts were imparted by the laying on of the Apostles hands (Acts 8:14-18).

Resurrection of the dead (v. 2). The resurrection of Christ gives us hope that all will be raised from the dead (1 Cor. 15:20-22).

Eternal judgment (v. 2). This is the final judgment that all men face that has eternal consequences (Heb. 9:27; 2 Cor. 5:10).

This we will do (v. 3). Going on to maturity can and will be done with God being our helper (John 15:5; Phil. 4:13). Opportunities to grow are made possible by God. "It also imparts the sense that the opportunities for the readers to achieve spiritual maturity may not be endless, and the time to be busy growing in the faith is now."[5]

Encouragement Due to the Dangers of Apostasy (vv. 4-8)

The warning here is that if one does not go on to maturity, it is possible to drift away to the point of no return. The author had previously warned them that one could reach the point of unbelief if he doesn't take heed (Heb. 3:12).

If you fall away it is impossible to renew (vv. 4-6). If one falls away (v. 6), it will be impossible to bring him to repentance. This is not describing one who drifts into sin and then turns back to God.[6] Rather, this is a picture of a complete apostate who has renounced the Christ. If one allowed the pressures of persecution to cause him to turn back to Judaism, he would be turning his back on the Lord Jesus Christ.

One thing that makes it impossible is that they turn away from what they already knew to be the truth. They were once enlightened (v.4).[7] They became Christians and were in the light (Eph. 5:8; Col. 1:13). They tasted of (experienced, enjoyed) the heavenly gift (salvation and spiritual blessings). They were partakers of the Holy Spirit (v. 4) which probably refers to the indwelling of the Holy Spirit (Rom. 8:9-11). They tasted of the good word of God (v. 5). They had received the word, embracing it as "good." They also experienced the power of the age to come. The age to come refers to the age of the Messiah. The power may have reference to the power of the Spirit in revealing and confirming the truth. Or, it may

---

5   David McClister, *A Commentary on Hebrews*, 211.

6   Simon sinned and turned back to God (Acts 8:20-22). Peter did the same (Gal. 2:11-14).

7   Daniel H. King, Sr. argues that this is a reference to their baptism (*The Book of Hebrews*, Truth Commentaries, 177).

have reference to the power to save from sin. The point is that they had participated in the peculiar blessings of the Messianic age.[8]

It is impossible for them to return because they crucify the Son of God again and put him to an open shame (v. 6). That is, they have rejected the Christ and are thus in the same class as those who put him on the cross. They no longer have any trust or confidence in Christ. It is possible to so depart that we reach the point of no return.

End is to be burned (vv. 7-8). Here the author illustrates the consequence of apostasy with ground that is unproductive. A plot of ground that is fruitful receives a blessing from God (v. 7). It is spared from destruction. But, a field that produces thorns and briars is rejected and burned (v. 8). The application should be obvious. The Christian that is fruitful and productive (goes on to perfection) will be blessed of God. However, the Christian who falls away is like the field of briars that is "near to being cursed"[9] and will be burned. Apostasy has eternal consequences.

Encouragement Based on Confidence in the Hebrews (vv. 9-12)

Persuaded better things of the Hebrews (v. 9). This points back to being burned (v. 8). The writer is persuaded that will not happen to them. He has confidence that they will grow and progress. The "things that accompany salvation" refers to the maturity that goes with salvation that he expected to see from them. He has confidence in them even though "we speak in this manner" (v. 9). The warnings that are given doesn't mean that the author thinks they are not going to persevere.

You have worked and labored (v. 10). His confidence is based on what they had done in other areas and done quite well. They had cared for those in need. Since we believe this letter to be sent to the church at Jerusalem, the situations in Acts 2:44-46; 4:32-27 and 6:1-8 may be what the author had in mind.

Show the same diligence unto the end (vv. 11-12). He urges them to show the same diligence in other areas (such as growing in their knowledge and maturity) that they had shown in the area of benevolence. They are urged not to be sluggish[10], but rather follow the example of those who had endured through faith (v. 12). Abraham is such an example as seen in the following verses.

Encouragement Based on the Promises of God (vv. 13-20)

The writer now focuses on the promises of God. Like Abraham, the Hebrews can put their trust in the promises of God and persevere and be rewarded.

God's promises confirmed by an oath (vv. 13-18). When God makes a promise and confirms it with an oath there can be no greater assurance.

---

8   Theses verses obviously refute the Calvinistic doctrine of once saved always saved. One of the arguments the Calvinist makes is that if one falls away that is proof that he never was really saved in the first place. These verses show that is not the case.

9   "The fact that they are only *near* being cursed points to the fact that as long as one lives he may decide to repent" (McClister, *ibid.*, 221-222).

10   Lazy. This is the opposite of diligence in verse 11. This is the same word for "dull" (5:11).

Promise to Abraham was confirmed and received (vv. 13-15). God made a promise to Abraham and swore by himself since he couldn't swear by any greater (v. 13). His promise (found in Gen. 22:16-17) was "Surely blessing I will bless you, and multiplying I will multiply you." [11]

Abraham patiently waited on the fulfillment of his promise. "Abraham maintained his confidence in spite of the long and perplexing delay in the realization of God's **promise**. It must be remembered that his first child was born to him when he was one hundred years old, and a very long time after his wife could have expected to give birth to children. Moreover, his grandchildren were not born until he had attained the age of one hundred and sixty (Gen. 25:26), just fifteen years before his death (Gen. 25:7). Truly, he had **patiently endured.**"[12]

By the time of his death Abraham had seen enough of the promise being fulfilled that the writer could say he obtained the promise (v. 15). He saw enough to be assured of the rest being fulfilled.

Assured by two immutable things (vv. 16-18). When man gives an oath it is an appeal to a higher authority (God) in order to confirm what he has said. The intent is to end all argument or dispute (v. 16). Thus, God, wanting to show that his counsel (his promise) was immutable (unchangeable), he confirmed it by an oath (v. 17).

Since it is impossible for God to lie (v. 18), we have strong consolation by two immutable (unchangeable) things: God's promise and God's oath. We have the same assurance that Abraham had. Just as the guilty fled to the city of refuge to escape death (Num. 35), we have fled from the consequence of sin to the hope that is before us. That hope is assured by the promises of God.

Hope is the anchor of the soul (vv. 19-20). As an anchor is to a ship so is hope to our soul. It holds us sure and steadfast. Our anchor is fixed behind the veil (in heaven) where Christ, our forerunner[13], has gone and become our High Priest. With that, the author is ready to return to the subject of Christ being a High Priest after the order of Melchizedek (Chapter 7).

Use of the Old Testament in this Chapter	
Verse in Chapter 6	Old Testament Reference
v. 14	Genesis 22:16-17

---

11 "'Blessing I will bless' is a Hebraism, emphasizing the idea contained in the verb" (M. R. Vincent, *ibid.*).

12 King, *ibid.*, 192.

13 "An old word used for a spy, a scout, only here in the New Testament. Jesus has shown us the way, has gone on ahead, and is the surety *enguos* (NT:1450), Heb 7:22) and guarantor of our own entrance later" (A. T. Robertson, *Robertson's Word Pictures in the New Testament*, Electronic Database. Copyright (c) 1997 by Biblesoft & Robertson's Word Pictures in the New Testament. Copyright (c) 1985 by Broadman Press).

Questions

1. What are the "elementary principles of Christ" (v. 1)? Give evidence for your answer.

2. In what sense are we to "leave" the first principles?

3. What is the doctrine of baptisms (v. 2)?

4. Who is under consideration in verses 4-8 (the one that is impossible to bring to repentance)?

5. What makes it impossible for the one in verses 4-8 to repent?

6. What did the writer expect out of the Hebrews?

7. What had the Hebrew done in the past that gave the writer confidence in them?

8. What was the promise to Abraham?

9. What is the point about Abraham in verses 13-18?

10. What are the two immutable things (v. 18)?

Hebrews 7
The Priesthood Of Christ Is Superior To The Levitical
Lesson 7

Outline

I. Priesthood of Melchizedek Was Superior to the Levitical (vv. 1-10)

A. *Was king and priest* (v. 1a)

B. *Appointed priest – not through descent* (v. 3a)

C. *No predecessor or successor* (v. 3b)

D. *Abraham paid tithes to Melchizedek* (vv. 1b-2; 4-8)

E. *Levi (through Abraham) paid tithes to Melchizedek* (vv. 9-10)

II. A Change in Priesthood (vv. 11-19a)

A. *Because of imperfection of the Levitical priesthood* (v. 11)

B. *Required a change in the law* (vv. 12-19a)
1. For Christ was not of the tribe of Levi (vv. 12-14)
2. Yet, God said he would be priest (vv. 15-17)
3. Old law was annulled (vv. 18-19a)

III. Priesthood of Christ is Superior to the Levitical (vv. 19a-28)

A. *Because it provides better hope* (v. 19b)

B. *Because he was made priest by an oath* (vv. 20-22)

C. *Because he is a continual High Priest* (vv. 23-25)

D. *Because of his superior character* (vv. 26-28)

E. *Because of his superior offering* (v. 27)

Key Verse that Summarizes the Chapter

Hebrews 7:11

Therefore, if perfection were through the Levitical priesthood (for under it the people received the law), what further need was there that another priest should rise according to the order of Melchizedek, and not be called according to the order of Aaron?

Here the author takes up the subject of Christ being a High Priest after the order of Melchize-dek that he left off at Hebrews 5:10 as he launched into a warning about not maturing. Even though the Hebrews were lacking in maturity, he presses on with the subject that "is hard to explain" (Heb. 5:11).[1]

Priesthood of Melchizedek Was Superior to the Levitical (vv. 1-10)

The writer has previously stated that Christ is a High Priest after the order of Melchizedek (5:6-10; 6:20). His point in these ten verses is to show that the priesthood of Melchizedek was superior to the Levitical priesthood. Thus, if the priesthood of Christ is after the order of Melchizedek, then his priesthood is superior to the Levitical.

Was king and priest (v. 1a). Melchizedek is only mentioned twice in the Old Testament (Gen. 14:17-20; Psalms 110:4).[2] He was king of Salem[3] and priest of the Most High God.[4] No priest under the Levitical priesthood was king as well as priest.

Appointed priest – not through descent (v. 3a). "Without father, without mother, without genealogy, having neither beginning of days nor end of life" means that there is no record of his birth or his death. Thus, he did not become priest because of lineage or descent. In contrast, under the Levitical priesthood those who became High Priest were in the lineage of Aaron (Exo. 29:9, 29; Num. 25:12-13).[5] In this way, Melchizedek was made like the Son of God. "For it is very obvious that the Holy Spirit has intentionally thrown an impenetrable vail over both the birth and the death of Melchisedec, over both his parentage and his posterity, for the purpose of making him a more perfect type of Christ."[6]

No predecessor or successor (v. 3b). He remains a priest continually. That is, he had no predecessor or successor. His was a one-high-priest priesthood.

Abraham paid tithes to Melchizedek (vv. 1b-2; 4-8). As Abraham returned from the battle where he rescued Lot (Gen. 14:1-20), he met Melchizedek and received a blessing from him and then gave him a tithe (vv. 1b-2).

The name Melchizedek means "king of righteousness" (v. 2). Since the name Salem means peace, then being king of Salem means he is "king of peace". This indeed makes him a type of Christ.

These verses establish that Abraham acknowledged that Melchizedek was superior by two things: (1) giving a tithe to him, and (2) receiving a blessing from him. Abraham gave

---

1   The answer to immaturity is to push forward into the meat of the word.
2   The only mention of him in the New Testament is in three chapters of Hebrews (5, 6, 7).
3   "The general opinion among the Jews was that Salem was the same as Jerusalem, as stated by Josephus (Ant, I, x, 2), who adds (VII, iii, 2) that it was known as Solyma (Saluma, variants, according to Whiston, Salem and Hierosolyma) in the time of Abraham" (*International Standard Bible Encyclopaedia*, Electronic Database Copyright (c)1996 by Biblesoft). Also Psalms 76:2 equates Salem with Zion.
4   Jesus is king and priest (Zech. 6:12-13).
5   In the post-exile period some were excluded from being priest because their lineage could not be established (Ezra 2:61-62; Neh. 7:63-64).
6   Robert Milligan, *Vol. IX – Epistle to the Hebrews*, New Testament Commentary, 195.

a tenth of the spoils (v. 4).[7] The Levitical priest received tithes because it is commanded (Num. 18:21, 24, 26-29). Their ability to collect the tithe from their brethren was by the law and not based on superiority. However, there was no such law that Abraham had to give a tithe. Neither was there any kindred to the king of Salem. Thus, the basis for giving the tithe was superiority.

Melchizedek blessed Abraham (vv. 1b, 6, 7). He blessed him as a priest of God (one who had authority to bestow God's intended good upon another). The conclusion of the author is that the lesser is blessed by the greater (v. 7).

Under the Levitical priesthood tithes were paid to men who died and another priest took his place (v. 8). But, the picture of Melchizedek is that he lives (v. 8). Since there is no word on his death or the end of his priesthood, the record is that he lives.

Levi (through Abraham) paid tithes to Melchizedek (vv. 9-10). Since Levi was a descendant of Abraham, he (through Abraham) paid tithes to Melchizedek "so to speak."[8]

A Change in Priesthood (vv. 11-19a)

If Christ is a High Priest after the order of Melchizedek, then there has to be a change in the priesthood.

Because of imperfection of the Levitical priesthood (v. 11). A change was necessary because of the inability of the Levitical priesthood, with its sacrifices, to remove sin (cf. Heb. 10:4). "Under it the people received the law" that is, "on the basis of it the people received the law" (NASV). The Levitical priesthood was the basis of the law being given. Various regulations of the law were carried out by the priests. The priesthood and the law were inseparable.

The author proves his point about the imperfection of the Levitical priesthood by appealing to Psalm 110:4 (which he doesn't quote until verse 17). If the Levitical system had been perfect why would there be a need for another priest like Melchizedek as promised in the Psalm?

Required a change in the law (vv. 12-19a). Since the priesthood and the law are inseparable, a change in the priesthood requires a change in the law (v. 12).[9]

For Christ was not of the tribe of Levi (vv. 12-14). The reason the law had to be changed is that Christ was not from the tribe of Levi (v. 13). Rather, he arose[10] from the tribe of Judah "of which tribe Moses spoke nothing concerning priesthood" (v. 14).[11] The point is

---

7   Literally the top of heap, "chief spoils" (ASV), or "choicest spoils" (NASV).
8   "As I may so say-to preclude his words being taken in the mere literal sense; I may say virtually, Levi, in the person of his father Abraham, acknowledged Melchisedek's superiority, and paid tithes to him" (*Jamieson, Fausset, and Brown Commentary*, Electronic Database. Copyright (c) 1997 by Biblesoft).
9   This is a powerful point to make to those who claim we are still under the Old Testament. If the law has not changed, the priesthood has not changed (thus Christ is not our High Priest). If the priesthood changed, then the law has changed.
10 The KJV says "sprang" out of Judah. This is a reference to Christ being a Branch out of the root of Jesse (Isa. 11:1; Jer. 23:5,6; 33:15; Zech. 3:8; 6:12).
11 Here we learn the silence of God is not permissive, but prohibitive.

that Jesus, being from the tribe of Judah, could not be a priest under the Levitical system and the old law.

Yet, God said he would be priest (vv. 15-17). It is "far more evident" that the law must be changed when we consider that Christ was to be priest in the likeness of Melchizedek (v. 15). Christ did not become priest by "the law of fleshly commandment" (v. 16), that is by law of physical descent. He became High Priest by the power of an endless[12] life. The expression, "power of an endless life" is in contrast to the "fleshly commandment" (physical descent) that was just mentioned. The fact that Jesus is alive (since he was raised from the dead) enabled him to become High Priest.

The passage from which the author makes his point is Psalm 110:4. There God promised that he would be a priest. From that we have to conclude there must be a change in the law.

The idea of his being a priest *forever* is best explained by Robert Milligan, "As he is the only begotten Son of the Father, so also he is now the only king and high priest that is appointed by the Father; and as such he will set as a priest upon his throne until the purposes of God in reference to the redemption of mankind shall have been fully accomplished. Then, and not until then, will he deliver up both the kingdom and the priesthood to the Father. But that epoch, like the beginning of his administration, is concealed from the eyes of mortals. In the representation of his priesthood, therefore, as given by the Holy Spirit, there is neither beginning nor ending. Like Melchisedek, he abides a priest perpetually."[13]

Old law was annulled (vv. 18-19a). The old law has been annulled (set aside, NASV)[14] because of its "weakness and unprofitableness" and it "made nothing perfect". All three of these expressions describe the inability of the law to remove sin (cf. v. 11).

Priesthood of Christ is Superior to the Levitical (vv. 19a-28)

This section gets to the heart of what this chapter is saying—the priesthood of Christ is superior to the Levitical priesthood. He has already told us that Melchizedek's priesthood was superior to the Levitical (vv. 1-10) and that the priesthood of Christ is in the likeness of Melchizedek (vv. 15-17). Therefore, the priesthood of Christ is superior to the Levitical. Now the author gives us five reasons why the priesthood of Christ is so much better.

Because it provides better hope (v. 19b). The better hope is in contrast to the weakness and unprofitableness (v. 18) of the old priesthood and law. The priesthood of Christ does what the old could not do – it removes sin so that man can draw near to God.

Because he was made priest by an oath (vv. 20-22). The sons of Levi were made priest without an oath which shows that their priesthood was subject to change. Christ, however, was made High Priest with an oath (Psalm 110:4) which shows his priesthood was not subject to change.[15]

---

12 ESV translates this "indestructible."
13 *Ibid.*, 207-208.
14 The word translated "annulling" is used only here and in Hebrews 9:26 where it is translated "put away" with reference to sin.
15 "...it was God's purpose of old, even in the time of David, to set aside the Old Economy and introduce the New; thereby proving indirectly from Psa. cx 4, the very great superiority of Christ's priesthood over that of Aaron" (Milligan, *ibid.*, 209).

By this oath Jesus became a surety ("guarantor" ESV; "guarantee" NKJV footnote) of a better covenant. The promise of a different High Priest (Psalm 110:4) was a promise of a better covenant (since the priesthood and covenant are inseparable).[16]

Because he is a continual High Priest (vv. 23-25). There were many High Priests under the Levitical system for the simple reason that one would die and another took his place. In contrast, Jesus, because he lives forever, continues his priesthood. Being an unchangeable High Priest he is able to save to the uttermost (completely) because he is always living and making intercession for his people (v. 25).[17]

Because of his superior character (vv. 26-28). Jesus as our High Priest is "fitting for us" ("meets our need" NIV) because of his characteristics. He is **holy** (pious, devout, pure), **harmless** (innocent, blameless), **undefiled** (without spot or stain), **separate from sinners** (sinless and exalted above them), and **higher than the heavens** (passed through the heavens cf. 4:14).

Jesus does not need to daily offer sacrifices as those High Priest did (v 27).[18] "...this statement means that Jesus' daily intercession does not require a daily sacrifice, in contrast to the Levitical high priests who had to offer a sacrifice every time they approached God (even if it was only yearly). That is, 'daily' does not describe the duties of the high priests in the Levitical system, but simply refers to Jesus' high priesthood. As Guthrie explains, 'He has no need in his daily ministry to offer sacrifices for himself as those priests did.'"[19] This is because of his superior character – he is sinless (Heb. 4:15).

Note the contrast: the high priest of the old law were men who have weakness (v. 28). However Jesus has been perfected forever. Jesus was appointed by an oath (Psalm 110:4) which is more recent than the law pertaining to the Levitical priesthood, showing that God indeed intended to change the priesthood to one that is superior.

Because of his superior offering (v. 27). The sacrifice Christ offered as our High Priest is Himself, thus making his priesthood superior.

Use of the Old Testament in this Chapter	
Verse in Chapter 7	Old Testament Reference
v. 17	Psalm 110:4
v. 21	Psalm 110:4

---

16 The NIV renders verse 22: "Because of this oath, Jesus has become the guarantee of a better covenant."

17 As our High Priest, Jesus didn't just act on our behalf in the past (his sacrifice), but he is working on our behalf even now.

18 This verse is difficult. On the surface it seems to be saying that the high priests offered daily sacrifices (which the priests did, but not the high priests). One explanation could be that the high priest stood at the head of the Levitical system and had oversight of the daily sacrifices. Also, the daily sacrifices were for him (the high priest) as well as everyone else, for he was a sinner. However, the explanation given seems to better explain the text.

19 David McClister, *A Commentary on Hebrews*, 268-269.

Questions

1. Who was Melchizedek?

2. What does "Without father, without mother, without genealogy, having neither beginning of days nor end of life" (v. 3) mean?

3. What does the name Melchizedek mean?

4. What two things happened when Abraham met Melchizedek that prove that Melchizedek was superior?

5. How does Abraham paying tithes to Melchizedek prove that Melchizedek's priesthood is superior to the Levitical?

6. In what way was the Old Testament imperfect (v.11)?

7. Why did the law have to be changed?

8. What is the better hope that comes with a change in priesthood?

9. What does the oath (vv. 20-22) prove about the priesthood of Christ?

10. What characteristics of Christ does the Hebrew writer give that makes him superior to the Levitical priests?

Hebrews 8

Lesson 8
A Better Ministry And Covenant

Outline

I. **A Better Priesthood [Ministry]** (vv. 1-5)

    A. *We have a High Priest – Christ* (vv. 1-2)
       1. At the right hand of God (v. 1)
       2. A minister of the sanctuary and true tabernacle (v. 2)

    B. *He has an offering* (v. 3)

    C. *If he were on earth he couldn't be a priest* (vv. 4-5)
       1. There are priest (Levites) who offer gifts according to the law (v. 4)
       2. These priests are a copy and shadow of Christ's priesthood (v. 5)

II. **A Better Covenant** (vv. 6-13)

    A. *Better promises* (v. 6)

    B. *Fault with the first means there is need for another* (vv. 7-8a)

    C. *God promised through Jeremiah a new covenant* (vv. 8b-13)
       1. Created a different people (vv. 9-11)
          a. Not like their rebellious fathers (v. 9)
          b. The law shall be in their hearts and they will know God (vv. 10-11)
       2. Offers complete forgiveness (v. 12)

    D. *This one being new – makes the other old and obsolete* (v. 13)

Key Verse that Summarizes the Chapter

Hebrews 8:6

But now He has obtained a more excellent ministry, inasmuch as He is also Mediator of a better covenant, which was established on better promises.

The previous chapter had established that the priesthood of Christ is superior to the Levitical priesthood. There the author had introduced the idea that a change in priesthood required a change in the law (7:12). In this chapter, we see more about the superiority of his priesthood with an expansion of the idea of a better covenant.

A Better Priesthood [Ministry] (vv. 1-5)

We have a High Priest – Christ (vv. 1-2). The author begins with the main point[1] of what he is saying about the priesthood of Christ: We have a High Priest in Jesus Christ (v. 1). The reader has been lead through the evidence that he is qualified for the role (5:1-10), and that his priesthood is superior to the Levitical one (chapter 7). Now his point is that he is a High Priest in heaven and not on earth (vv. 1-5) and is a mediator of a better covenant (vv. 6-13).

Our High Priest is seated at the right hand of God (v. 1), a position of exaltation and power.[2] This was not true of any of the Aaronic priests. Christ is a minister of the sanctuary and true tabernacle[3] (v. 2). The term "minister" (a servant) as used here describes one who does the work of the High Priest. He serves in the sanctuary ("holies" NKJV footnote; "holy places" ESV) which is heaven. The tabernacle of this priesthood is the true tabernacle (as opposed to the copy or shadow). It (unlike the tabernacle in the Old Testament) was erected by God and not man (v. 2). Thus, it is superior.

He has an offering (v. 3). The function of a High Priest is to offer sacrifices (cf. 5:1). Jesus being our high priest has an offering – the sacrifice of himself (cf. 7:27).

If he were on earth he could not be a priest (vv. 4-5). The point in these two verses is that Christ is a priest in heaven and not on earth. He could not be a priest on earth for he was not of the tribe of Levi (cf. 7:11-14). Since Christ is a High Priest and has a sacrifice, it is either earthly or heavenly. There are priests (Levites) who offer gifts (earthly offerings) according to the law (v. 4).Thus, his offering is heavenly.

The Levitical priesthood was a copy and shadow of Christ's priesthood (v. 5). "Copy" ("representation" ESV; "example" KJV) suggest that the previous priesthood was not the real or true, but merely a type or representation of the real. A "shadow" (like a man's shadow on the ground) is an image or representation of the real thing.[4]

As proof of his point, the author cites Exodus 25:40 where Moses was instructed to make the tabernacle according to the pattern. If the tabernacle (which was a copy, type or model of the real) was made according to the pattern, it then is a true representation of the real. To illustrate: Suppose you are going to build a new house. You get an architect to draw blueprints (a pattern). But, before you go to the contractor to have the house built, you take the blueprints to a model maker to have him build a to-scale model of the house. Only when the model is according to the pattern is it a true model or type of the real. The tabernacle Moses built was not the real, but a copy (model) of the real.

---

1   The ASV: "chief point".
2   If he is at the right hand of God in heaven, then he is not a priest on earth (cf. v. 4).
3   This is the first reference to the tabernacle in the book of Hebrews.
4   This would be a hard pill to swallow for the Jew who had thought the Levitcal priest-hood was to continue.

A Better Covenant (vv. 6-13)

Now that Christ is a High Priest, he has obtained a more excellent (better, superior) ministry.[5] The ESV renders verse 6, "But as it is, Christ has obtained a ministry that is as much more excellent than the old as the covenant he mediates is better, since it is enacted on better promises."

A change in priesthood required a change in the law (cf. 7:12), which also demands a change in a mediator. A mediator is "a go-between"[6] who officiates between two parties (God and man). Moses was the mediator of the Old Covenant (Gal. 3:19-20; Exo. 20:19-21). Christ is the mediator of the new and better covenant.

Better promises (v. 6). The New Covenant is established on better promises. The promises are better in content, not that they are more reliable than any promise under the old. The details of those promises will be seen in the following verses.

Fault with the first means there is need for another (vv. 7-8a). The fault with the first covenant was that it could not (and was not designed to) bring complete forgiveness (cf. Gal. 3:21). "In one sense, the Old Covenant was just as perfect as the New. Each of them was perfectly adapted to the end for which it was designed. But the former never did and never could justify, sanctify, or save any one. In these respects it was relatively faulty, and the New is faultless."[7] Since the first had fault, there was a need for a new covenant.

Verse 8 says, "finding fault with them"[8] was the basis for the promise he quotes from Jeremiah. The fault was that those under the law failed to keep it (cf. v. 9).

God promised through Jeremiah a new covenant (vv. 8b-13). The author quotes Jeremiah 31:31-34 which promised a new[9] covenant. The fact that God promised a new covenant says that there was fault with the first.

The promise was given to the house of Israel and the house of Jacob (v. 8), a reference to all of God's people. In verse 10 he uses the terms "house of Israel" to describe the same people. This promise was "not with them as separate distinct houses, nor even as tribes; but simply as individuals. All tribal and family distinctions are now lost in Israel; and all who enter into covenant with God become members of the one household of faith..."[10]

Jeremiah's prophecy had two major points:

1. Created a different people (vv. 9-11). The point of these three verses is that the New Covenant will create a different people. They will not be like their rebellious fathers (v. 9).

---

5   Compare verse 2, "Minister of the sanctuary..."
6   W. E. Vine, *Vine's Expository Dictionary of New Testament Words.*
7   Robert Milligan, *Vol. IX – Epistle to the Hebrews*, New Testament Commentary, 226.
8   NIV says, "found fault with the people."
9   The word here means not only new in reference to time, but new "as to form or quality, of different nature from what is contrasted as old" (W.E. Vine, *Vine's Expository Dictionary of Biblical Words*, Copyright (c)1985, Thomas Nelson Publishers).
10   Milligan, *ibid.*, 229.

"This new Israel would be all that the old Israel was not."[11] Israel of old rebelled and did not keep the covenant (v. 9). Thus, God rejected them. "It had now become manifest that by the Old Covenant no flesh could be justified before God: for the people were continually violating its requirements, and consequently God was under the necessity, so to speak, of rejecting them."[12]

Under the new, the law will be in their hearts and they will know God (vv. 10-11). "The Israel of old never really adopted God's ways for themselves. God had given them his instructions for how they were to live, but they did not appropriate them, they did not allow those commandments to mold them into the image God wanted them to have. The law was therefore always something that was external to them. In the new relationship with the new Israel, however, things would be different. The new Israel would internalize God's demands...It is this inward commitment, which makes obedience meaningful, that would be the basis of the new covenant with God."[13]

With such inward commitment, God said, "I will be their God, and they shall be My people" (v. 10).[14] This describes their loyalty to God through which they become his special treasure. Under the new covenant, they shall know the Lord (v. 11).[15] Under the old, one became a part of Israel by birth (involuntary). Though already a part of Israel, they had to be taught to know the Lord. In contrast, under the new, one has to be taught to be a part of Israel (cf. John 6:45), thus voluntary.

2. Offers complete forgiveness (v. 12). Sin under the Old Covenant was remembered again every year (cf. 10:3). Under the new, complete forgiveness is promised where God remembers the sin no more. This is what the old could not do.

The one being new – makes the other old and obsolete (v. 13). Since God promised a "new" covenant, this means the previous one is "old" and obsolete (no longer binding). God himself testified (through Jeremiah) that the Old Testament was not intended to be final. The author's use of the Old Testament quotations is most interesting here.[16] He makes similar points from Psalm 95, Psalm 110, and Jeremiah 31. In chapters 3-4 he shows Psalm 95 was written *after* Joshua led the people into Canaan, which shows that the promised rest was not fully obtained. In chapters 5 and 7 he shows that Psalm 110:4 was written *after* the institution of the Levitical priesthood, which shows a change in priesthood was intended. Likewise, Jeremiah 31 was written *after* the establishment of the old covenant, which shows the coming of a new covenant.

Use of the Old Testament in this Chapter	
Verse in Chapter 8	Old Testament Reference
v. 5	Exodus 25:40
vv. 8-12	Jeremiah 31:31-34

---

11 David McClister, *A Commentary on Hebrews*, 284.
12 Milligan, *ibid.*, 233.
13 McClister, *ibid.*, 289.
14 Compare Exodus 6:7; Hosea 2:23; and Zechariah 8:8.
15 This is more than knowing who God is. It is a close relationship of knowing him very well (cf. Gal. 4:8-9).
16 Credit to McClister for the development of this point (*ibid.*, 284).

Questions

1. What is the "main point" (v. 1)?

2. What is the sanctuary (v. 2)?

3. What is the true tabernacle?

4. Why could Christ not be a priest on earth (v. 4)?

5. What point is the author making when he quotes Exodus 25:40?

6. What is a mediator (v. 6)?

7. What was the fault of the Old Testament?

8. What does "finding fault with them" (v. 8) mean?

9. Jeremiah's prophecy had two major points. What were they?

10. What is the contrast or difference in forgiveness under the old law and the new?

Hebrews 9

Lesson 9
The First Covenant - A Type Of The New

Outline

I. **The Tabernacle of the First Covenant Pointed to the Better** (vv. 1-10)

    A. *The Tabernacle of the First Covenant* (vv. 1-5)
        1. First covenant had ordinances (v. 1)
        2. The Sanctuary (v. 2)
        3. The Holiest of all (vv. 3-5)

    B. *Services of the first pointed to the better* (vv. 6-10)
        1. Services of the first (vv. 6-7)
            a. Priests' function (v. 6)
            b. High priest's function (v. 7)
        2. The first was a figure of the better to come (vv. 8-10)

II. **Eternal Redemption by a Greater High Priest and Tabernacle** (vv. 11-14)

    A. *Christ is the High Priest of a greater tabernacle* (v. 11)

    B. *Eternal redemption* (vv. 12-14)

III. **Christ is the Mediator of the New Covenant** (vv. 15-22)

    A. *By his death* (vv. 15a, 16-17)

    B. *Obtained redemption for those under the first covenant* (v. 15b)

    C. *New covenant dedicated by blood like the first* (vv. 18-22)

IV. **The Better and Perfect High Priest** (vv. 23-28)

    A. *Christ entered into heaven (Holiest of All) for us* (vv. 23-24)

    B. *Christ offered a one-time sacrifice* (vv. 25-28)
        1. Sacrifice of the Old Covenant – often and with the blood of another (v. 25)
        2. Sacrifice of Christ – once with the sacrifice of himself (vv. 26-28)

```
┌─────────────────────────────────────────────────────────────────┐
│ ════════════  Key Verse that Summarizes the Chapter  ════════════ │
│                                                                   │
│                          Hebrews 9:24                             │
│  For Christ has not entered the holy places made with hands, which│
│  are copies of the true, but into heaven itself, now to appear in │
│  the presence of God for us.                                      │
└─────────────────────────────────────────────────────────────────┘
```

The point of this chapter is to show that the old priesthood with its covenant was divinely established and divinely annulled. The author had just pointed out from Jeremiah that it was God ("He says", 8:13) who said a new covenant was coming, thus the old was obsolete. The first verse of this chapter shows the first had ordinances of *divine* service. Thus, the old was divinely established and divinely made obsolete.

When we get through with this chapter there is not a whole lot of information that has not already been touched upon or at least hinted at in previous chapters. So why does the author labor so long in so many chapters driving home the point about the priesthood of Christ? No doubt the prejudice in religious matters (that is always extremely difficult to address) was as strong here as it would be in our own day. Thus, with patient and methodical argumentation our author makes his case.

One of the obstacles that kept some from understanding about the superiority of the priesthood of Christ is the failure to see the first for what God intended it to be – a type or shadow of the real to come. This chapter makes that clear.

The Tabernacle of the First Covenant Pointed to the Better (vv. 1-10)

The tabernacle of the first covenant (vv. 1-5). Why does the author speak of the tabernacle rather than the Temple (which was still standing)? Perhaps for several reasons. One, the tabernacle gave way to the Temple (something more permanent) which shows that it and the whole system was temporary. Second, he goes back to the first sanctuary and Holy Place when all that was intended to be there was there. By the time Solomon dedicated the temple, Aaron's rod and the pot of manna were missing from the ark (1 Kings 8:9; 2 Chron. 5:10).

The first covenant had ordinances of divine service (v. 1). Again, what the writer said about the old is not said to reject the old (as if it wasn't from God), but to show that God designed it to be a type of the new. The first had the earthly sanctuary[1] in contrast to the heavenly.

The tabernacle had two compartments (Exo. 26:33). The first part is here called the sanctuary (v. 2) containing the lampstand (Exo. 25:31-40; 26:35; 27:20-21) and the table of showbread (Exo. 25:23-30). The showbread was twelve cakes in two stacks of six (Lev. 24:5-9).

The second part, beyond the second veil, was called the Holiest of all (v. 3; Exo. 26:31-25). The text says concerning the most holy place, "which had the golden censer" (v. 4). This, no doubt, refers to the altar of incense which was actually just outside the veil in the sanctuary (1 Kings 6:22). Some translations render this "golden altar of incense" (ASV, NASV, NIV, ESV). The altar of incense (Exo. 30:1-10) was omitted in the list at verse 2. Thus, this reference (v. 4) is probably it. Furthermore, the text doesn't say that this "golden censer" was actually

---

1   ASV: "a sanctuary of this world".

inside the Holiest of all. Rather, it "had" the golden censer or altar of incense. That is, it pertained to the Holiest of all or was just outside the veil.

This second part had the ark of the covenant (Exo. 25:10-16) which contained the golden pot of manna, Aaron's rod that budded and the tablets of the covenant (v. 4). Over the top of the ark were two cherubims (Exo. 25:17-22) that overshadowed the mercy seat.[2]

Services of the first pointed to the better (vv. 6-10). The point of these verses is to show that what took place in the service of the first tabernacle was a figure of the better to come. Services of the first tabernacle involved the priests going into the sanctuary to perform their services (v. 6). Their work included keeping the lamps burning (Exo. 27:20-21), burning incense morning and evening (Exo. 30:7-8), changing the loaves every Sabbath (Lev. 24:5-8), and sprinkling blood before the altar (Lev. 4:6).

Only the high priest entered the second part (Holiest of All) which he did once a year (Lev. 16)[3]. He took the blood of bulls and goats and entered the Holiest of All to offer the blood for himself and the people (v. 7).

The first was a figure of the better to come (vv. 8-10). The fact that only the high priest could enter through the veil, demonstrated that the way into the Holiest of All (heaven) had not been made known (v. 8). When Jesus died on the cross, the veil of the temple was torn in two from top to bottom (Matt. 27:51). Thus, the way (through his death) had been made known.

The services of the first tabernacle were merely symbolic ("figure" KJV, ASV) of something greater to come (v. 9). The sacrifices offered then could not perfect the conscience (could not completely purge the sin) because the sins were remembered again every year (cf. 10:3).

The first covenant and service "concerned only"[4] with food, drinks, various washings and fleshly ordinances (v. 10). Rather than being able to make the conscience clean, the old law dealt with what could and could not be eaten (Lev. 11), drinks (perhaps the drink offerings of Numbers 28), and various washings (which included the high priest washing on the day of atonement – Lev. 16:4, 24). These were all fleshly or carnal ordinances. "They pertained to 'fleshly' issues rather than to those things which purify the inner man, in this instance, the conscience (see also 7:5 and 15)."[5]

The first was temporary for it was to last until the time of reformation or change (the time of Christ, cf. v. 11).

---

2   The mercy seat is where man met with God (Exo. 25:22). The word translated "mercy seat" is translated "propitiation" (Rom. 3:25).

3   That doesn't mean that he only made one trip through the veil on that day. In fact, he made at least three trips. First, he entered with incense (Lev. 16:12-13). Second, he entered with the blood of the bullock (Lev. 16:14). Third, he entered with the blood of a goat (Lev. 16:15).

4   ESV: "deal only with" and ASV: "being only (with meats, drinks and divers washings) carnal ordinances".

5   Daniel H. King, Sr., *The Book of Hebrews*, Truth Commentaries, 270.

Eternal Redemption by a Greater High Priest and Tabernacle (vv. 11-14)

Christ is the High Priest of a greater tabernacle (v. 11). The first tablernalce and priesthood pointed to the priesthood of Christ and a more perfect tabernacle (not made by human hands as the first). This priesthood can do what the first could not.

Eternal redemption (vv. 12-14). The sacrifice of Christ was also a blood sacrifice, but not the blood of animals (v. 12). Rather, he entered through the veil[6] with his own blood, by which he obtained eternal redemption.[7] The author argues that if the blood of bulls and goats with the ashes of a heifer[8] could accomplish an outward purifying[9], how much more could the blood of Christ (who is eternal in his nature – deity, and without spot) cleanse the conscience from dead works[10] (vv. 13-14).

Christ is the Mediator of the New Covenant (vv. 15-22)

The previous chapter had introduced the idea that the change in the priesthood and the law means a change in the mediator (8:6). Here the author expands on that concept.

By his death (vv. 15a, 16-17). The death of Christ is the means by which the New Covenant became effective and Christ is made the mediator of it (v. 15a). The author illustrates with a will or testament (vv. 16-17). When one writes a will, it is not effective until the person dies. It has no force at all while the testator lives. So, the last will and testament of Christ became effective by his death.

Obtained redemption for those under the first covenant (v. 15b). Through his death, Christ obtained eternal redemption for those who lived under the first covenant (cf. Rom. 3:25). The point is to show how effective the sacrifice of Christ is in contrast to the sacrifices under the old covenant. Those sacrifices could not take away the sin of those who lived under the old. However, the sacrifice of Christ can do more than temporarily remove the sin, it obtained eternal redemption for those in the future and those that came before.

New covenant dedicated by blood like the first (vv. 18-22). The point here is that just as the Old Covenant was dedicated (inaugurated, ESV, NASV) by blood, so the New Covenant was dedicated by the blood of Christ. The writer is referring to the account in Exodus 24:1-8.[11]

---

6   Not only did Jesus die for our sins, but he had to be raised to offer his blood in heaven. That is the sense in which we are saved by his life (Rom. 5:10). He was raised for our justification (Rom. 4:25).
7   The redemption is eternal in contrast to the inability of the first to completely take away sin (10:3). Through the blood of Christ, God will remember the sin no more (8:12). Christ is the author of eternal salvation (5:9).
8   The ashes of a heifer were used in the water of purification (Num. 19:2-10).
9   That is the purification accomplished under the old never was complete – the conscience was never cleansed.
10   Dead works are works (actions) that lead to death. All sin does that.
11   Comparing Exodus 24 with Hebrews 9, one will notice some difference. Exodus does not mention goats. Exodus says that Moses put half the blood on the altar and half on the people (24:6, 8), whereas Hebrews says he also sprinkled it on the book (v. 19). Exodus does not mention the water, scarlet wool and hyssop. Both texts are recorded by inspiration and can be harmonized.

Let us not miss the main point while focusing on the differences. "The essential part of the whole ceremony being the 'blood-shedding,' it is of no importance for the general argument that the account in Exodus is not exactly followed."[12]

The tabernacle was sprinkled as well (v. 21). This had to be at a different time than the covenant being dedicated because the tabernacle was not yet built (Exo. 40).[13]

The writer adds, "almost all things were purified with blood" (v. 22) since there were some things purified by water and fire (Num. 31:22-24; Lev. 15:10). Yet one thing that always required blood was the sacrifice for sin – "without shedding of blood there is no remission" (v. 22). The reason being - that life is in the blood (Lev. 17).

The Better and Perfect High Priest (vv. 23-28)

Christ entered into heaven (Holiest of All) for us (vv. 23-24). If that which is the copy of the true had to be purified with blood (v. 22), the heavenly things[14] should be purified with better sacrifices (v. 23). Thus, Christ has entered into the Holiest of All (heaven) to offer his sacrifice before God (v. 24).

Christ offered a one-time sacrifice (vv. 25-28). The high priests under the Old Covenant made their sacrifices often (every year) with the blood of another – an animal (v. 25). In contrast, at the end of the ages,[15] Christ offers his sacrifice *once* with this own blood (v. 26). Just as every man dies once, so Christ dies once (vv. 27-28). There is no need for him to suffer again.

To those who eagerly wait for him, he will appear a second time for salvation. That is, when the second coming occurs he will complete his work by taking his faithful to heaven. He will come "apart from sin" (v. 28). That is, he will not come to bear the sin of man for that work was accomplished with his first coming.

Use of the Old Testament in this Chapter	
Verse in Chapter 9	Old Testament Reference
v. 20	Exodus 24:8

---

12 H. D. M. Spence-Jones, *Hebrews,* 234. *Pulpit Commentary,* London; New York: Funk & Wagnalls Company.

13 Exodus 40 does not mention the use of blood, only the anointing with oil.

14 This is a reference to the spiritual in contrast to the fleshly. "It is not that heaven itself is or was in a state of impurity, but rather that sinful men cannot gain access to that holy place until their sin problem has been permanently resolved" (King, *ibid.,* 288-289).

15 In the last days (cf. 1:2).

Questions

1. Why does the author speak of the tabernacle rather than the Temple (which was still standing)?

2. What is the significance of the mercy seat?

3. What did the Holy Spirit indicate and how did he indicate it?

4. What is the time of reformation (v. 11)?

5. What did Jesus passing through the veil into the Holiest of All have to do with our salvation (v. 12)?

6. How did Jesus become the mediator of the New Covenant?

7. Why were blood sacrifices offered?

8. What is the point of verse 27? How does man dying once fit the context?

9. What is the author saying when he uses the expression "apart from sin" (v. 28)?

10. What is the main point of chapter 9?

Hebrews 10

Lesson 10
Sacrifices And Exhortations

Hebrews 10

I. The Sacrifices Contrasted (vv. 1-18)

    A. *The Levitical system was not sufficient* (vv. 1-4)
       1. Not the image, but the shadow (v. 1)
       2. Remembrance made of sin every year (v. 3)
       3. Could not forgive sin (vv. 1, 2, 4)

    B. *Christ's offering is all sufficient* (vv. 5-18)
       1. Fulfills the will of God (vv. 5-10a)
       2. Absolute forgiveness obtained (vv. 10b-18)

II. Exhortation to Steadfastness (vv. 19-39)

    A. *Exhortation to greater diligence* (vv. 19-25)
       1. Based on cleansing through Christ (vv. 19-22)
       2. What greater diligence involves (vv. 23-25)

    B. *Exhortation based upon the danger of apostasy* (vv. 26-31)

    C. *Exhortation based upon past endurance* (vv. 32-34)

    D. *Exhortation based upon receiving the promise* (vv. 35-39)

Key Verse that Summarizes the Chapter

Hebrews 10:11
And every priest stands ministering daily and offering repeatedly the same sacrifices, which can never take away sins.

The chapter serves as a transition from the first major section (Christ is the Way -1:1 -10:18) to the second (Don't Give Up – 10:19 – 13:28).[1] In the first eighteen verses the writer contrast the sacrifices. Though the major point is the same that has been made in the previous chapters, he develops some points that have not been introduced thus far. Having concluded his arguments showing that Christ is the way, the author begins the application portion of the book with the fourth of five warning sections of the book (vv. 19-39).

---

1   See the outline of the book in the Introduction.

The Sacrifices Contrasted (vv. 1-18)

The Levitical system was not sufficient (vv. 1-4). The point of these first four verses is to show what the sacrifices under the old law could and could not accomplish.

Not the image, but the shadow (v. 1). The old covenant with its sacrifices was merely a shadow (cf. 8:5) of the greater to come. The idea is that the old foreshadowed the new. "The word *shadow* here refers to a rough outline of anything, a mere sketch, such as a carpenter draws with a piece of chalk, or such as an artist delineates when he is about to make a picture. He sketches an outline of the object which he desires to draw, which has *some* resemblance to it, but is not the 'very image;' for it is not yet complete. The words rendered 'the very image' refer to a painting or statue which is finished, where every part is an exact copy of the original. The 'good things to come' here refer to the future bless-ings which would be conferred on man by the gospel. The idea is, that under the ancient sacrifices there was an imperfect representation; a dim outline of the blessings which the gospel would impart to men."[2]

Robertson observes that "shadow" can mean the shade that is cast by light, "The contrast here between σκια [*skia*] (shadow, shade caused by interruption of light as by trees, Mark 4:32) and εικων [*eikōn*] (image or picture) is striking."[3] The point is that the old with its sacrifices was not the true image, but merely a resemblance of the true.

Remembrance made of sin every year (v. 3). When the High Priest offered the sacrifice on the Day of Atonement (Lev. 16), it served to remind the worshippers that their sin was not completely removed. There was still a "consciousness of sin" (cf. v. 3). The sin was still there, for the blood of animals could not take it away (v. 4).[4] Note also the contrast to the sacrifice of Christ wherein God will remember the sins no more (v. 17).

Could not forgive sin (vv. 1, 2, 4). The fact that the sacrifices were repeatedly offered says that those sacrifices could not take away the sin (v. 1). If the animal sacrifices had completely removed the sin, there would be no need to continually offer them every year (v. 2). The blood of bulls and goats could not take away the sin (v. 4).[5]

Christ's offering is all sufficient (vv. 5-18). Here the contrast is drawn to the insufficient sacrifices in the previous verses.

Fulfills the will of God (vv. 5-10a). The writer quotes Psalm 40:6-8. Though taking his reference from the Septuagint, "The quotation does not agree with either the Hebrew

---

2   Albert Barnes, *Notes on the New Testament: Hebrews.* (R. Frew, Ed.), 218. London: Blackie & Son.

3   A. T. Robertson, *Word Pictures in the New Testament* (Heb. 10:1). Nashville, TN: Broadman Press.

4   "The cultic rights actually brought past sins into the present (cf. Lev. 16:21; Philo, The Special Laws 1.1215)" (Daniel H. King, Sr., *The Book of Hebrews*, Truth Commentaries, 300).

5   God has always demanded a blood sacrifice for life is in the blood (Lev. 17). The only perfect blood sacrifice would be the sacrifice of God's Son. Furthermore, the fol-lowing verses (vv. 5-10) will show that the sacrifice of Christ was a willing sacrifice whereas the animals were sacrificed against their will.

or the LXX, and the Hebrew and LXX do not agree."[6] The point of the Psalm is a call for genuine obedience to the will of God. Where Psalms says, "My ears You have opened" the Hebrews reference has "But a body You have prepared for me." The open ears has reference to willingly yielding to God's will. Christ was given a body so he could obey the will of God.

The use the writer makes of the Psalm is summarized in verses 8-10. God was not pleased with the sacrifices of the Old Covenant in the sense that they did not remove the sin (v. 8). But, Christ came (in the flesh) to fulfill God's plan for redeeming man (vv. 9-10a). In so doing, he took away the first system to establish the second (v. 9).[7]

Absolute forgiveness obtained (vv. 10b-18). Under the Levitical system the priests *stand* (indicating their work is incomplete) and continually offer sacrifices that do not take away sin (v. 11). In contrast, Christ offered one sacrifice and then *sat down* (indicating his work is finished) at the right hand of God (v. 12). By that one offering those being sanctified are perfected (complete forgiveness) forever (v. 14). The Holy Spirit gives witness (from Jer. 31:33-34)[8] to the power of the sacrifice of Christ in saying that their sins would be remembered no more (vv. 15-17). When there is complete remission of sin, there is no need for another offering (v. 18).

Exhortation to Steadfastness (vv. 19-39)

With these verses we begin the second major section of the book which we have entitled, "Don't Give Up" (10:19 – 13:28).[9] In light of the foundation that has been laid in the first section, the reader is urged to keep on the track they know to be right and don't give up. Also this begins the second section of this chapter. Here we have encouragement to be steadfast. We are informed of what that involves and the reasons for it. Note also, that these verses (vv. 19-39) consist of the fourth of the five warning sections in the book.[10]

Exhortation to greater diligence (vv. 19-25). We can now have boldness (confidence, ESV) to enter the Holiest (Heaven).[11] This assurance is based on the cleansing that is available through Christ (vv. 19-22). If the blood of Christ accomplished what the old sacrifices could not, then we can have the utmost confidence. We have access by a "new and living way" (v. 20). It is new in that it is fresh or recent (as opposed to the old). It is living as opposed to the lifeless entrance (way) into the most holy place of the tabernacle. It may refer to the life that is imparted by this way. However, Lenksi's approach is interesting, "...this way is 'living' because it consists of Christ himself who is 'the Way and the Life' (John 14:6), a way that is itself active and bears those who step upon it. We go farther than to say that it is 'living' because of its *connection* with the living Christ; the living Christ *is himself* the living way."[12] This new and living way is consecrated for us through the veil, his flesh (v. 22). Just as the veil of the tabernacle was the means of access into the most holy place, so through the

---

6   M. R. Vincent, *Word Studies in the New Testament*, 4:496. New York: Charles Scribner's Sons.

7   Man cannot be under two differing systems of law at the same time.

8   This is evidence that Jeremiah was inspired by the Holy Spirit.

9   See the outline of the book in the Introduction.

10 Look back at the Introduction for a list of the warning sections.

11 While this would include our entrance into heaven in eternity, here he seems to have reference to our approach to the throne of God as in Hebrews 4:14-16.

12 R. C. H. Lenski, *The Interpretation of the Epistle to the Hebrews and of the Epistle of James*, 344–345. Columbus, OH: Lutheran Book Concern.

flesh of Christ (his death) do we have access to the most holy place. Since this is true, we should draw near with a true heart (sincere, genuine) in full assurance (without any doubt, full trust in our High Priest) (v. 22). That boldness and assurance comes because our hearts are sprinkled from an evil conscience[13] (our hearts are cleansed of sin) and our bodies washed in pure water (been baptized).[14]

Now the author tells us what greater diligence involves (vv. 23-25). First, it involves **holding fast** to the "hope we profess" (NIV). Second, it involves **considering one another** in order to **stir up** (stimulate, NASB) love and good works (v. 24). Third, it includes **not forsaking the assembling** of the saints (v. 25). Fourth, it involves **exhorting one another** (v. 25).

Several points need to be observed about verse 25. The assembling refers to the act of assembling as evidenced by "as is the manner of some." Forsaking does not just include a complete abandonment, but even a one-time neglect.[15] The day approaching refers to the destruction of Jerusalem rather than the second coming for there were signs that indicated that it was nearing (Matt. 24). Such an event would be a great trial of their faith.

Some were already in the habit (ESV) of forsaking the assembling. What was the reason? We are either not told or the historical and textual context points to persecution. Later in the chapter he reminds them of enduring persecution in the past as evidence they can endure now (vv. 33-34). The resistance (12:4) they are facing is called a chastening of the Lord (12:1-6) that is peculiar to the sons of God (12:6). That is persecution that greatly discouraged some of these Christians (12:12). Barnes observed, "Some may have been deterred by the fear of persecution, as those who were thus assembled would be more exposed to danger than others."[16] The point for us is that if persecution was not to keep them from assembling, how does that compare with the reasons for forsaking today?

Exhortation based upon the danger of apostasy (vv. 26-31). If the Hebrews don't press on, there is the danger of falling away and losing their souls. If one willfully sins after becoming a child of God, he rejects the only sacrifice that will save – there will not be another (v. 26). Rather, he can look toward judgment with fear (v. 27) for he is worthy of worse punishment than one received under Moses (vv. 28-29). To apostatize is to trample the Son of God, count his blood an unholy or a common thing and insult the Holy Spirit (v. 29). The author makes his point by quoting Deuteronomy 32:35-36 which says that the Lord will punish those who turn from him (v. 30). His conclusion is that "It is a fearful thing to fall into the hand of the living God" (v. 31).

Exhortation based upon past endurance (vv. 32-34). The fact that the recipients of this book had endured persecution in the past says that they can endure the present opposition. They had been made a spectacle by reproaches and tribulations (v. 33),[17] suffered along

---

13 Compare Hebrews 9:13-14.

14 Baptism is referred to as a washing in other texts (Acts 22:16; Tit. 3:5). "Pure" does not refer to sanitary conditions of the water, but that it is not mixed with ashes as in Numbers 19.

15 The same word is found in Matthew 27:46 and 2 Timothy 4:16.

16 Albert Barnes, *Notes on the New Testament: Hebrews*. (R. Frew, Ed.), 234. London: Blackie & Son.

17 The ESV says, "publicly exposed to reproach and afflictions". The NIV says, "publicly exposed to insult and persecution."

with those in prison, and experienced the plundering of their property (v. 34). This they accepted with joy knowing that they had a better and enduring possession in heaven (v. 34).

Exhortation based upon receiving the promise (vv. 35-39). The readers are urged not to cast their confidence aside (which they would do if they turn back to Judaism) because they have a great reward (v. 35). If they would endure, doing the will of God, they will receive the promise (v. 36).[18]

As proof of his point, the writer quotes Habakkuk 2:3-4[19] (vv. 37-38). The coming of God (v. 37) is a coming in judgment. In Habakkuk the reference was to Babylon. Here, the author uses it to refer to Rome coming in the destruction of Jerusalem which was not far away from the time of the writing of this book. "The just shall live by faith" is explained in the next phrase and next verse. Rather than drawing back to destruction, we believe (keep on believing) to the saving of the soul.

Use of the Old Testament in this Chapter	
Verse in Chapter 10	Old Testament Reference
vv. 5-7	Psalm 40:6-8
v. 8	Psalm 40:6
v. 9	Psalm 40:7-8
v. 16	Jer. 31:33-34
v. 20	Deut. 32:35-36
vv. 37-38	Hab. 2:3-4

---

18 The promise is eternal life. It is the same as the "saving of the soul" (v. 39).
19 The quotation is from the Septuagint translation (LXX).

Questions

1. What are the two major sections of the book and how do they relate to each other?

2. What does it mean that the Old Covenant and its sacrifices were a "shadow" of the new?

3. In what sense was there a remembrance of sin every year (v. 3)?

4. Hebrews 10 quotes Psalm 40. The Psalm reference says, "My ears You have opened" while the Hebrews reference has "But a body You have prepared for me." What do those expressions have to do with each other?

5. What is the point being made from Psalm 40?

6. What is the contrast drawn in verses 11-12?

7. In what sense is the flesh of Christ a veil?

8. What four things are listed in this chapter that are involved in greater diligence?

9. What was causing some to forsake the assembling of the saints? What does that say to us today?

10. How is the expression, "the just shall live by faith" used by the Hebrew writer?

Hebrews 11

Lesson 11
Examples Of Faith

Outline

I. **The Nature of Faith** (vv. 1-3)

    A. *What faith is* (v. 1)

    B. *The power of faith* (vv. 2-3)

II. **Examples of Faith and its Power** (vv. 4-38)

    A. *Abel* (v. 4)

    B. *Enoch* (vv. 5-6)

    C. *Noah* (v. 7)

    D. *Abraham* (vv. 8-10, 12-19)
        1. Obeyed – went to a country (vv. 8-10)
        2. Believed the promise (vv. 11-12)
        3. Sacrificed his son (vv. 17-19)

    E. *Sarah* (v. 11)

    F. *These all died in faith looking for a better country* (vv. 13-16)

    G. *Isaac* (v. 20)

    H. *Jacob* (v. 21)

    I. *Joseph* (v. 21)

    J. *Moses* (vv. 23-29)

    K. *Walls of Jericho* (v. 30)

    L. *Rahab* (v. 31)

    M. *Other examples in general* (vv. 32-39)

III. **We Have Something Better** (vv. 39-40)

    A. *These did not received the promise* (v. 39)

    B. *God provided something better for us* (v. 40)

```
┌─────────────────────────────────────────────────────────────────┐
│═══════════ Key Verses that Summarizes the Chapter ═══════════     │
│                                                                   │
│                        Hebrews 11:39-40                           │
│ And all these, having obtained a good testimony through faith,    │
│ did not receive the promise,                                      │
│ God having provided something better for us, that they should     │
│ not be made perfect apart from us.                                │
└─────────────────────────────────────────────────────────────────┘
```

This chapter naturally flows out of the last part of chapter 10 where the writer urged his reader to hold on to the promises of God (vv. 35-39). There he told them not to cast away their confidence (v. 35), but keep on believing to the saving of the soul (v. 39). Here, we see examples of faith and see its power. "People of faith, because of the nature of faith itself, do not quit."[1] Thus, these great heroes of faith become the "cloud of witness" (12:1) that cheer us on as we run our own race.

The Nature of Faith (vv. 1-3)

Before looking at the examples, our author treats us to an understanding of the nature of faith. When one sees what faith is, what it does and its power (exemplified), he better appreciates the need for holding on to his own faith.

What it is (v. 1). While this verse is not a dictionary definition of faith, it defines faith nonetheless by describing what faith does. "There is scarcely any verse of the New Testament more important than this, for it states what is the nature of all true faith, and is the only definition of it which is attempted in the Scriptures."[2]

The substance of things hoped for. "*Substance*, as used by these translators, is *substantial nature*; the real nature of a thing which underlies and supports its outward form or properties."[3] It is "what stands under anything (a building, a contract, a promise)."[4] When the Christian has hope "beneath that anticipation lies a firm belief or trust that the thing not yet possessed actually exists and that its possession is certainly attainable."[5]

"Assurance" (ASV, ESV) gives the idea being expressed. Through faith, we can be sure of the things we hope for. Perhaps this is parallel to the phrase, "He is a rewarder of those who diligently seek Him" (v. 6).

Evidence of things not seen. "The word often signifies a process of proof or demonstration. So yon Soden: 'a being convinced. Therefore not a rash, feebly-grounded hypothesis,

---

1   David McClister, *A Commentary on Hebrews*, 380.
2   Albert Barnes, *Notes on the New Testament: Hebrews*, (R. Frew, Ed.), 248. London: Blackie & Son.
3   M. R. Vincent, *Word Studies in the New Testament*, 4:510. New York: Charles Scribner's Sons.
4   A. T. Robertson, *Word Pictures in the New Testament* (Heb 11:1). Nashville, TN: Broadman Press.
5   McClister, *ibid*, 382.

a dream of hope, the child of a wish.'"[6] "Conviction" (ASV, ESV) or "confidence" (NKJV fn) gives the idea being expressed. Faith involves "being convinced of what we do not see."[7] What he doesn't see would include God himself as well as the eternal home (cf. 2 Cor. 4:18). Perhaps the phrase, "believe that he is" (v. 6) would be parallel.

While the Christian does not see his eternal home, he is just as convinced of its reality as if he had already received it. "It is in this sense of 'confidence' or boldness that our author says that faith serves as a kind of proof"[8] of things not seen.

"Together the two statements in this verse define faith as something that connects the present to the future."[9] Perhaps this translation summarizes the points being made, "Faith means being sure of the things we hope for and knowing that something is real even if we do not see it" (NCV).

The power of faith (vv. 2-3). By faith the elders (those listed in this chapter) obtained a good testimony ("received their commendation" ESV).[10] By faith we understand that the worlds (universe, ESV) were created by the word of God. What we see now did not come from matter that already existed. By faith we are able to understand something that we did not see – the creation of the universe. We understand because we believe what God said (Gen. 1-2).

Examples of Faith and its Power (vv. 4-38)

Abel (v. 4). Abel offered the firstborn of his flock while Cain brought an offering of the fruit of the ground (Gen. 4:3-5). The Lord was pleased with Abel's sacrifice and not Cain's. The difference was that Abel offered his sacrifice "by faith" which means he followed the direction of God.[11] Because of his faith, he was declared to be righteous. Even though Abel is dead, he still speaks today through his example of faith.

Enoch (vv. 5-6). Enoch (like Elijah, 2 Kings 2:17) did not die, but was taken into heaven. The record is found in Genesis 5:24 which is quoted here. Before his translation, he had testimony that he pleased God.[12] Pleasing God is impossible without faith (v. 6), thus Enoch had faith.

One who comes to God must believe that he exist and believe he rewards those who diligently seek him (v. 6).[13] This is the faith that is required to sustain the Hebrews and us as well.

Noah (v. 7). By faith Noah built the ark because he was warned of God about the flood and destruction that he could not yet see (Gen. 6-9). At the time he was instructed to build the ark, this took great faith because there was no natural indication that such a flood would

---

6   M. R. Vincent, *ibid.*
7   *The NET Bible* (Heb 11:1). Biblical Studies Press.
8   McClister, *ibid,* 382.
9   McClister, *ibid,* 382.
10   Compare this verse with verse 39 where the author tell us who the elders were by pointing back to "all these" just mentioned.
11   This is because faith comes by hearing and hearing by the word of God (Rom. 10:17).
12   He walked with God (Gen. 5:24).
13   Here we see there is a difference in believing *in* God and *believing* God.

occur. There had never been one before. Because of his faith he condemned the world (by his example)[14] and was counted among the righteous.

Abraham (vv. 8-10, 12-19). No greater example of faith can be found than that of Abraham. Three things are stated in these verses that he did by faith: obeyed, believed, and sacrificed.

Obeyed (went to a country) (vv. 8-10). God called Abraham and told him to leave his home and travel to a far country where he had never been (Gen. 12:1-4). He obeyed! The reason he was able to be satisfied in a foreign land (v. 9) was that he looked toward a better and permanent home in heaven (v. 10).

Believed the promise (vv. 11-12). God told Abraham and Sarah that they would have a child even though both were very aged (Gen. 15:5-6; 17:1, 15-19; 18:9-15). Abraham believed the promise being fully convinced that God would do what he said (Rom. 4:16-21). Though Abraham was as good as dead (because of his age), a great multitude came from him (v. 12).

Sacrificed his son (vv. 17-19). Perhaps Abraham's greatest test of faith was when God told him to sacrifice his son Isaac (Gen. 22:1-19). Isaac was the one through whom God promised the seed (v. 18; Gen. 21:12). Abraham attempted to sacrifice his son thinking that God could raise him from the dead to fulfill his promise. When God prevented him from killing his son, Abraham figuratively received him from the dead (v. 19).

Sarah (v. 11). Like Abraham, Sarah believed the promise of a son. Though she was well past child bearing years, she was able to have a son because she trusted God who promised a son.

These all died in faith looking for a better country (vv. 13-16). "These" (those listed in verses 4-12) died with great faith even though they did not see the fulfillment of the promises made to them (v. 13). By faith they were able to see the fulfillment, though it was far off (v. 13). They considered themselves as pilgrims and strangers which implies they were looking for a better (heavenly) country (vv. 14, 16). If they had considered the land God had given Abraham the fullness of the promises of God, they might have gone back to the Ur of the Chaldees. They certainly had opportunity. They didn't for they set their eyes toward heaven. Such faith pleased God (v. 16b).

Isaac (v. 20). Isaac blessed Jacob and Esau (Gen. 27:26-40). The point here is not about how Jacob deceived Isaac and took away the blessing intended for Esau, but how Isaac looked by faith to the future fulfillment of the blessing he pronounced.

Jacob (v. 21). The author refers to two events near the end of Jacob's life where his faith looked to the future. He first mentions Jacob blessed the sons of Joseph, Manasseh and Ephraim (Gen. 48:1-22). Again the details are not the point here, but the fact that in the blessing Jacob's faith in God's fulfillment in the future is seen. The second event (Gen. 47:27-31) is when Joseph swore to his father that he would not bury him in Egypt. Jacob's faith is seen in his bowing in worship (Gen. 47:31).[15]

---

14 Compare Matthew 12:41-42.
15 "Leaning on the top of his staff" is taken from the LXX translation of Genesis 47:31. The word could be staff or bed.

Joseph (v. 21). Joseph, because he was fully persuaded that the people of God would come into the land that was promised, made his brethren swear they would bring his bones with them (Gen. 50:24).

Moses (vv. 23-29). There are five points that are given here about Moses, all of which point to the power of faith.

1. Was hid three months (v. 23). This verse speaks of the faith of Moses' parents who were seeking to save Moses' life through their confidence in God (Exo. 2:2).

2. Chose the people of God (vv. 24-26). When Moses became of age,[16] he faced the choice of remaining with the Egyptians (as the son of Pharaoh's daughter) and enjoy the riches of Egypt or suffer with the people of God.[17] He chose the latter because his faith looked to the reward.

3. Forsook Egypt (v. 27). Moses fled from Egypt and went to Midian after he killed the Egyptian (Exo. 2:11-25). Though Moses did have fear (Exo. 2:14), he overcame that fear and endured for his faith focused on God (whom he could not see) rather than the king he could see.

4. Kept the Passover (v. 28). When the Passover was instituted (Exo. 12:1-28), God required that blood be sprinkled on the doorpost lest the firstborn should be killed. This required faith in two ways. First, they believed God that the firstborn were going to die. Second, they believed that putting blood on the door would keep their firstborn from dying.[18] Moses kept the Passover because he had faith.

5. Passed through the Red Sea (v. 29). Because of faith, Moses and the children of Israel were able to pass through the Red Sea on dry ground (Exo. 14:22). It took faith to walk between the walls of water on either side. The reference to the Egyptians drowning shows the effects of not having faith.

Walls of Jericho (v. 30). The city of Jericho was taken in the conquest because Joshua and the people of God had faith to do what God said (Josh. 6).

Rahab (v. 31). Rahab was spared from the destruction of Jericho because of her faith. When she hid the spies, she stated her faith in God (Josh. 2:9-11).

Other examples in general (vv. 32-39). Here the author groups many other examples of faith together for time and space would not permit details about each one. He mentions Gideon (Jud. 6-8), Barak (Jud. 4-5), Samson (Jud. 13-16), Jephthah (Jud. 11-12), David (1 Sam. 16-31; 2 Sam.), and Samuel (1 Sam. 1-25) by name. Then the author gives a long list of things that were either accomplished or endured through faith. Space in this little work will not permit comment on each expression. However, we list just four. Some stopped the

---

16 Forty years old (Acts 7:23).
17 This suffering is called "the reproach of Christ" (v. 26) because Christ and his followers have suffered the same type of reproach (insult, disgrace). Every follower of Christ is faced with the same choice that Moses faced.
18 McClister, *ibid.*, 418.

mouths of lions (Jud. 14:6; 1 Sam. 17:34; Dan. 6:22), quenched the violence of fire (Dan. 3:25), received their dead raised to life (1 Kings 17:22; 2 Kings 4:35-37) and sawn in two.[19]

We Have Something Better (vv. 39-40)

These did not receive the promise (v 39). All those that are either mentioned or alluded to in this chapter received a good report because of their faith. However, they did not live to see the fulfillment of the promise of the Messiah.

God provided something better for us (v. 40). The something better would be the better covenant, better priesthood and better sacrifice. Through the better things that we have in Christ, these Old Testament worthies can be made perfect (complete forgiveness) along with us.[20]

Use of the Old Testament in this Chapter	
Verse in Chapter 11	Old Testament Reference
v. 5	Gen. 5:24
v. 18	Gen. 21:12

---

19 Jewish tradition says Isaiah was sawn in two.
20 See Hebrew 9:15 and Romans 3:25.

Questions

1. How does chapter 11 relate to chapter 10?

2. What does "substance of things hoped for" (v. 1) mean?

3. What does "evidence of things not seen" (v. 1) mean?

4. How does one's faith relate to creation (v. 2)?

5. What was the difference in the sacrifices offered by Cain and Abel?

6. What three things did Abraham do because of his faith?

7. What does "these all died in faith" (v. 13) mean?

8. What does "the reproach of Christ" (v. 26) mean?

9. Keeping the Passover (v. 28) required faith in what two ways?

10. For class discussion: How did faith work in the lives of all those mentioned in this chapter? How should that impact the Hebrews?

Hebrews 12

Lesson 12
Exhortation To Have
The Same Faith And Endurance

Outline

I. **Exhortation to Continue in the Course** (vv. 1-3)

    A. *From the example of many who have gone before* (v. 1)

    B. *From the example of the Lord* (vv. 2-3)

II. **Exhortation to Endure Afflictions Patiently (vv. 4-11)**

    A. *In view of their comparative lightness* (v. 4)

    B. *In view of the fact that the chastening of the Lord is intended for our good* (vv. 5-11)

III. **Exhortation to Greater Zeal – Lest We Lose It All** (vv. 12-17)

    A. *Stir greater zeal and strength* (vv. 12-13)

    B. *Follow peace and holiness* (v. 14)

    C. *Look carefully* (vv. 15-17)

IV. **Exhortation Based on the Nature of the New Economy** (vv. 18-29)

    A. *Superior honors and blessings of the new* (vv. 18-24)

    B. *The authoritative voice of God* (vv. 25-26)

    C. *A remaining and stable kingdom* (vv. 27-29)

Key Verse that Summarizes the Chapter

Hebrews 12:1

Therefore we also, since we are surrounded by so great a cloud of witnesses, let us lay aside every weight, and the sin which so easily ensnares us, and let us run with endurance the race that is set before us.

This chapter consist of the fifth and final warning section of the book.[1] Here the admonition is to have the same faith as those heroes of faith in the previous chapter lest one fall short of the grace of God (cf. v. 15). The reader is encouraged to stay the course (vv. 1-3), endure the persecution patiently (vv. 4-11), have greater zeal (vv. 12-17), and consider the nature of the new economy (vv. 18-29).

Exhortation to Continue in the Course (vv. 1-3)

From the example of many who have gone before (v. 1). The writer pictures the Christian life as running a race. To encourage the runners, they are reminded of the great cloud of witnesses (those people of faith mentioned in the previous chapter) that surround them. "The metaphor refers to the great amphitheatre with the arena for the runners and the tiers upon tiers of seats rising up like a cloud. The μαρτυρες [*martures*] (word of witnesses, DVR) here are not mere spectators (θεαται [*theatai*]), but testifiers (witnesses) who testify from their own experience (11:2, 4, 5, 33, 39) to God's fulfilling his promises as shown in chapter 11.[2] As we run, we look to the stands and see those who have already run, endured and won. This tells us we can do the same and encourages us to keep running. As we run, we must lay aside any weight hindering the run. Every sin and hindrance to our service must be laid aside. Then the race must be run with endurance—not giving up under the pressure of persecution (cf. 10:36).

From the example of the Lord (vv. 2-3). The runner is encouraged to focus attention on Jesus who is the author[3] and finisher[4] of our faith. "He is the founder of faith not in the sense that he was the first person to have faith in God, but that he was the first one to finish the course of faith all the way to heaven itself and to receive his heavenly reward... He has blazed the full length of the trail before us, showing us the way to reach that same goal ourselves (cf. 2:10)."[5]

Jesus is the perfect example of running the race with endurance. He endured the shame of the cross (v. 2) and hostility[6] from sinners (v. 3) and then sat down at the right hand of God. His focus on the joy of the future enabled him to endure all the opposition. If we do not look to Jesus and follow his example, we can become weary and discouraged. This picture "appears to be that of the runner letting himself get tired of the effort and thus quitting."[7]

Exhortation to Endure Afflictions Patiently (vv. 4-11)

The recipients of this book were facing persecution. They needed words of encouragement to help them press on to the end. Here the writer says they could endure in view of two things:

---

1 Go back to the Introduction to see the five sections.
2 A. T. Robertson, *Word Pictures in the New Testament* (Heb 12:1). Nashville, TN: Broadman Press.
3 NKJV footnote: "originator." ESV: "founder." Same word for "captain" (2:10).
4 NKJV footnote and ESV: "perfecter."
5 David McClister, *A Commentary on Hebrew*, 444.
6 ASV: "gainsaying."
7 R. C. H. Lenski, *The Interpretation of the Epistle to the Hebrews and of the Epistle of James*, 431. Columbus, OH: Lutheran Book Concern.

In view of their comparative lightness (v. 4). Whatever they have endured thus far, they had not yet paid the ultimate sacrifice of blood. Jesus did, as well as Stephen (Acts 7) and James (Acts 12).

In view of the fact that the chastening of the Lord is intended for our good (vv. 5-11). Here the writer quotes Proverbs 3:11-12 and makes application about the chastening[8] of the Lord. This refers to persecution for it is suffering that is peculiar to the sons of God (v. 6). It is "of the Lord" in the sense that God allows it for our good (in the same way he sends a strong delusion, 2 Thess. 2:10-12).

The reader is urged not be discouraged by the afflictions they face (vv. 5-6), for God, because he loves his children (v. 6), allows it. Just as our earthly fathers corrected us, so God chastens his children through the persecution (vv. 6-8). God's design in allowing it is the good that comes from it (vv. 9-11). When our earthly fathers disciplined us, we paid them respect (v. 9). Likewise we should willingly submit to our father who disciplines us (v. 9). The suffering in persecution should not drive one from God, but rather toward God. One who has been "trained" (v. 11) by this chastening is a partaker of God's holiness and is righteous (vv. 10-11). The suffering makes one stronger. Thus, one can endure persecution when he realizes good will come from it.

Exhortation to Greater Zeal – Lest We Lose It All (vv. 12-17)

Here the readers are warned that if they don't have greater zeal and endurance they will lose it all.

Stir greater zeal and strength (vv. 12-13). The hands hanging down and knees becoming feeble (taken from Isa. 35:3) is a picture of tired, weary, weak and discouraged people. They are almost ready to throw up their hands and quit. Instead, "They were to make every effort to bear up under their trials. The hope of victory will do much to strengthen one almost exhausted in battle; the desire to reach home invigorates the frame of the weary traveler."[9]

"Make the straight paths for your feet" (v. 13) means "keep on the right path" (NCV). "It has the sense of following the path that leads straight to the goal, without taking any deviation from it."[10] If this is not done, that which is lame[11] will be completely dislocated (disabled, NIV). Here is the idea of losing it all without greater zeal and strength.

Follow peace and holiness (v. 14).[12] The admonition is to pursue peace with all (which is part of making straight paths). This certainly includes the world and brethren. But, how does this fit the context which deals with persecution? "Rather than retaliate in kind, God's people are to react to mistreatment in a peaceful way...We react with peace because we believe that God's way is best for us."[13]

---

8   The word translated "chastening" is translated "training" (Eph. 6:4) and "instruction" (2 Tim. 3:16).
9   Albert Barnes, *Notes on the New Testament: Hebrews*. (R. Frew, Ed.), 300. London: Blackie & Son.
10 McClister, *ibid.*, 458.
11 Same word is translated "cripple" (Acts 14:8).
12 The writer is possibly alluding to Psalm 34:14.
13 McClister, *ibid.*, 459.

The admonition also says pursue holiness.[14] Whether under persecution or not, God's people must always seek to be pure. Peace should not be sought at the expense of holiness. Without peace and holiness, one will not see the Lord. Here again is the idea of losing it all without greater zeal and strength.

Look carefully (vv. 15-17). While pursuing peace and holiness we must "look carefully"[15] or given close attention to others as well as ourselves.[16] This is to be done lest anyone of four things should happen:

1. Lest anyone fall short of the grace of God (v. 15). It is possible that under the pressure of persecution one would be discouraged and give up and thus fall short of the heavenly home provided by God's grace.

2. Lest any root of bitterness springing up cause trouble (v. 15). The writer is referencing Deuteronomy 29:18 where Moses warns about being overtaken in sin. "The allusion, in both cases, is to a bitter plant springing up among those that were cultivated for ornament or use, or to a tree bearing bitter and poisonous fruit, among those that produced good fruit. The reference of the apostle is to some person who should produce a similar effect in the church—to one who should inculcate false doctrines; or who should apostatize; or who should lead an unholy life, and thus be the means of corrupting and destroying others. They were to be at especial pains that no such person should start up from among themselves, or be tolerated by them."[17]

3. Lest there be any fornicator (v. 16). A fornicator is given to sensual pleasures. He is focused on physical and earthly over the spiritual and heavenly things.

4. Lest there be any profane person (vv. 16-17). Esau is given as an example of a profane ("unholy", ESV; "godless" fn. NKJV) person who did not regard God or his religion. He like the fornicator[18] followed his fleshly desires in selling his birthright (Gen. 25:27-34). He later found no place for repentance which means he could not change Isaac's mind. The NCV helps to paraphrase verse 17: "You remember that after Esau did this, he wanted to get his father's blessing, but his father refused. Esau could find no way to change what he had done, even though he wanted the blessing so much that he cried."

If we do not have greater zeal and strength (which involves watching out for our fellow Christians), we (them and us) could lose it all.

Exhortation Based on the Nature of the New Economy (vv. 18-29)

Superior honors and blessings of the new (vv. 18-24). "For" (v. 18) points back to the responsibilities just mentioned. The fact that we are under a superior covenant gives us reason

---

14 Strong's defines this "*purification*, i.e. (the state) *purity.*"
15 The word translated "looking carefully" is only used two times in the New Testament: Here and 1 Peter 5:2 where it is used of elders "serving as overseers."
16 ESV: "See to it that no one fails to obtain the grace of God..."
17 Albert Barnes, *ibid.*, 302.
18 Some interpret the text as saying Esau was a fornicator (using the term figuratively). The text is not saying Esau was a fornicator but that he (being profane) and the fornicator are alike. Both are worldly, focusing on fleshly desires.

to strive for greater zeal and endurance. "To enforce the considerations already urged, the apostle introduces this sublime comparison between the old and new dispensations; vers. 18–24. The object, in accordance with the principal scope of the epistle, is, to guard them against apostasy. To do this, he shows that under the new dispensation there was much more to bind them to fidelity, and to make apostasy dangerous, than there was under the old."[19]

Description of the old (vv. 18-21). The expressions here describes the awe and terror that filled the hearts of those who approached the mountain. "The purpose of the writer is to contrast the experience of coming before God in the new and old covenants."[20] Sinai was a mount that could not be touched (Exo. 19:10-13), was burned with fire (Exo. 19:18; Deut. 4:11), was covered with blackness and darkness (Exo. 19:16). There was the blast of the trumpet (Exo. 19:19) and the voice of God (Exo. 19:19). It was so fearful that those who heard the voice begged that the word not be spoken to them anymore (Exo. 20:18-19).

Verse 20 quotes Exodus 19:12-13. Verse 21 quotes Deuteronomy 9:19. The point of both is the terror that was experienced by the people and Moses.

Description of the new (vv. 22-24). The expressions used here describe both what is experienced now and what awaits the people of God in the future. In coming to God, instead of coming to Mount Sinai they have come to Mount Zion, also called the city of the living God, the heavenly Jerusalem (heaven, Rev. 21-22). Rather than coming to an earthly mount, they have come to a heavenly mount. There is an innumerable (myraids, YLT) company of angels gathered around the throne of God ready to welcome the faithful of God.

Those coming to God come to a general assembly ("festal gathering" NKJV fn) that is the church that is made up of those who hold the rank and privilege of the firstborn who have their names registered in heaven. Additionally they have come to God (judge of all), to the spirits of those who through the ages have been perfected by the blood of Christ (v 23), to Jesus the Mediator, and to the blood of Christ that is better than the blood Abel shed in his sacrifice.

The authoritative voice of God (vv. 25-26). Because of the superior nature of the new covenant, we should listen to the voice of God. If one who refused to listen to Moses was punished, how much more will we not escape if we refuse to listen to Christ (v. 25). The same voice of God that shook Mount Sinai (Exo. 19:18) has promised to shake the earth and heavens also (Hag. 2:6).[21]

A remaining and stable kingdom (vv. 27-29). The author makes application of the text he just quoted. The contrast here is between things that can be shaken (removed) and things that cannot be shaken (cannot be removed). The things being shaken would be the Old Covenant with its priesthood and sacrifices.[22] In contrast we have received a kingdom which cannot be shaken (cf. Dan. 2:44). Therefore, "let us be grateful for receiving" such a kingdom

---

19 Albert Barnes, *Notes on the New Testament: Hebrews.* (R. Frew, Ed.), 305. London: Blackie & Son.

20 Daniel H. King, Sr., *The Book of Hebrews, Truth Commentaries*, 432.

21 This refers to the overthrow of nations or change in order.

22 Jerusalem itself will be destroyed within a short time of the writing of this book.

(ESV)[23] and thus serve God with reverence and godly fear because God is a consuming fire[24] (will punish the disobedient).

Use of the Old Testament in this Chapter	
Verse in Chapter 12	Old Testament Reference
vv. 5-6	Prov. 3:11-12
v. 12	Isa. 35:3
v. 20	Exo. 19:12-13
v. 21	Deut. 9:19
vv. 26-27	Hag. 2:6

23 The NKJV says "let us have grace"; NASB: "let us show gratitude".
24 Compare Exodus 24:17.

Questions

1. How does this chapter relate to the previous chapter?

2. What is the "cloud of witness" (v.1)?

3. What does it mean that Jesus is the author and finisher of our faith?

4. In what way could the persecution be considered light (v. 4)?

5. What is the chastening of the Lord (vv. 5-11)?

6. What is the point being made about the chastening of the Lord?

7. What does following "peace" have to do with things in the context?

8. What is meant by looking carefully (v. 15)?

9. What is the contrast in verses 18-24?

10. What has been shaken and what will not be shaken?

Hebrews 13

Lesson 13
Some Final And Practical Exhortations

Outline

I. Some Personal Responsibilities (vv. 1-7)

   A. *Brotherly love* (v. 1)

   B. *Hospitality* (v. 2)

   C. *Remember those in prison* (v. 3)

   D. *Faithfulness in marriage* (v. 4)

   E. *Contentment -vs- covetousness* (vv. 5-6)

   F. *Remember and follow leaders* (v. 7)

II. Continue in the Service of Christ (vv. 8-16)

   A. *Jesus is unchangeable* (v. 8)

   B. *Make a clear break from Judaism* (vv. 9-14)
      1. Don't be carried away by error (v. 9)
      2. Must leave "Jerusalem" to go to Christ (vv. 10-14)

   C. *The sacrifices we offer* (vv. 15-16)
      1. Continually (v. 15)
      2. We offer: (vv. 15-16)
         a. Praise (v. 15)
         b. Doing good (v. 16)
         c. Sharing (v. 16)
      3. God is well pleased (v. 16)

III. Duties toward Elders and Other Servants (vv. 17-19)

   A. *Obey and submit to elders* (v. 17)

   B. *Pray for Paul and others* (vv. 18-19)

IV. Prayer for the Hebrews that They May be Complete Doing God's Will (vv. 20-21)

   A. *Final Remarks* (vv. 22-25)

   B. *Heed exhortations* (v. 22)

   C. *Timothy is set free* (v. 23)

   D. *Salutations to the Hebrews from those in Italy* (v. 24)

   E. *Grace unto them* (v. 25)

```
┌─────────────────────────────────────────────────────────────┐
│ ══════ Key Verse that Summarizes the Chapter ══════          │
│                                                               │
│                      Hebrews 13:3                             │
│  Therefore let us go forth to Him, outside the camp, bearing  │
│  His reproach.                                                │
└─────────────────────────────────────────────────────────────┘
```

This last chapter deals with some final and practical points of putting faith into practice. Rather than being an appendix to the book it serves as more of a summary of the book.

Some Personal Responsibilities (vv. 1-7)

Brotherly love[1] (v. 1). This is not a general love that we are to have for all men, rather "the peculiar love of Christians to each other as brethren."[2] In the midst of persecution some might have the tendency to let their love decline, thus becoming indifferent toward brethren. The writer is not suggesting that this has already happened, but merely warning that it should continue. This love will be demonstrated in showing hospitality (v. 2), remembering those in prison (v. 3), and remembering those who are mistreated (v. 3).

Hospitality (v. 2). "Entertain strangers" is translated "hospitality" in the ESV and in Romans 12:13. There would be Christians traveling from one place to another to preach or because of the pressure of persecution (cf. Acts 8:1-4) who would need a place to stay. The writer adds that some who did so unknowingly entertained angels (Gen. 18:1-2; 19:1). The point is that at the time, Abraham did not know these men were angels. Likewise, we may show hospitality toward some without knowing the great blessing we will receive. "The influence of such guests in a family is worth more than it costs to entertain them."[3]

Remember those in prison (v. 3). Though others may be included, the context would point to those who are in prison because of persecution. It is possible that some felt it dangerous to be identified with those in prison lest they too be mistreated. One should consider himself as if he is in prison with them. Additionally those who are mistreated should be remembered.[4] This should be done in view of the fact that you are in the body also. That is, since you are still alive you may become the subject of such suffering as well.

Faithfulness in marriage (v. 4). Marriage is honorable[5] and the bed (sexual relationship within the marriage) is pure. Yet, fornication (sexual union before marriage) and adultery (sexual union outside of marriage) God will condemn. Here and in the next two verses the author addresses two areas where focus on earthly pleasures could pull one away from God.

---

1   From the Greek word *philadelphia*.
2   H.D.M. Spence-Jones, (Ed.). Hebrews, 393. *Pulpit Commentary*. London; New York: Funk & Wagnalls Company.
3   Albert Barnes, *Notes on the New Testament: Hebrews*. (R. Frew, Ed.), 314. London: Blackie & Son.
4   Probably refers to those who are mistreated through persecution, though not imprisoned.
5   Lenki and other writers suggest that the writer is defending marriage against the false asceticism that considered the marriage bed (sexual union) defiling and filthy.

Contentment -vs- covetousness (vv. 5-6). The ESV translates this "Keep your life free from the love of money..." (cf. ASV). Under persecution some Christians suffered the loss of possessions (cf. 10:34). One whose love for the material causes him to cling to his earthly things may have a real struggle under persecution. The child of God should be content ("satisfied with what you have", NCV) for God has promised not to leave or forsake.[6] We may lose possessions, but we still have what is important. Since that is true, we can say the Lord is our helper and we don't fear what man can do (v. 6).[7] Man can take away our material goods, but the Lord is ever with us.

Remember and follow leaders (v. 7). Those who rule over you ("leaders", ESV) would certainly include elders (cf. vv. 17, 24), but would seem to embrace more. This probably refers to leaders who have passed on before.[8] Remember what they taught from the word and follow their example knowing the end result.[9]

Continue in the Service of Christ (vv. 8-16)

The point in these verses is to press on in the service of God and not turn back to Judaism. They serve well as a summary of what the whole book is about.

Jesus is unchangeable (v. 8). In contrast to the changing leadership in the church (as one generation passes on), Jesus never changes. There is no reason to leave Christ since nothing has changed.

Make a clear break from Judaism (vv. 9-14). This unit of verses simply urges the Hebrews to make a clear break from Judaism and thus continue to serve Christ. They should not allow the strange doctrines (such as Judaism) to lead them astray (v. 9). One's relationship to God is established by grace (that provided the sacrifice of Christ) instead of the foods (standing for regulations of the Old Testament law). The later did not profit (bring salvation) to those who kept those laws.

The next five verses say one must leave "Jerusalem" (Judaism) to go to Christ (vv. 10-14). The altar (sacrifice) of Christ cannot benefit those who serve the tabernacle, that is, those under Judaism (v. 10). The reason is given in the verses that follow. Under the Old Testament the bodies of the sacrificed animals were burned outside of the camp (v 11).[10] Likewise Jesus suffered the cross outside the gate (v. 12). Thus, one who wants to benefit from the sacrifice of Christ must go outside the camp (leave "Jerusalem" or Judaism) accepting the reproach (suffering) that goes with it (v. 13). Jerusalem (and Judaism) is not a continuing

---

6   Taken from Deuteronomy 31:6, Joshua 1:5, and 1 Chronicles 28:20.
7   Taken from Psalm 27:1, and 118:6.
8   In contrast to the unchanging Christ (v. 8).
9   We learn something very practical about being a leader from this verse. They lead by the teaching of the word and by a great example. If you want to be a leader (whether you are ever an elder, preacher or teacher), fill your heart with the word and be a positive example.
10 "In the case of many Jewish sacrifices, portions of the animals offered in sacrifice were later eaten by the priests (Leviticus 4:22-35, 6:25-26). But the flesh of any sin offering whose blood was carried into the Holy of Holies by the high priest on the Day of Atonement was not to be eaten. Instead it was to be carried outside the camp and there entirely consumed by fire (Leviticus 16:27)" (Gareth L. Reese, *Hebrews*, 240).

(abiding, ASV) city, but we seek such a city to come (v. 14). Jerusalem would be destroyed in just a few short years after this epistle was written.[11]

The sacrifices we offer (vv. 15-16). In the service of Christ we are to continually offer sacrifices to God (v. 15). Three sacrifices[12] are listed in these two verses: praise (v. 15), doing good (v. 16), and sharing[13] (v. 16). God is well pleased with such sacrifices (v. 16).

Duties toward Elders and Other Servants (vv. 17-19)

Obey and submit to elders (v. 17). Those who rule over you would be the elders of the local church who have oversight (Acts 20:28; 1 Pet. 5:1-4). The members have the responsibility to submit to the elder's lead. The reason given is that elders are watching for their souls, recognizing they will give an account for their work. We should be respectful and cooperative with the elders so that their work is that of joy and not grief.

Pray for Paul and others (vv. 18-19). The writer (whom we think to be Paul) urged the readers to pray for him and his companions. Even though his rebuke has been strong, he reminds them they should pray for him because all he has done has been with a pure conscience (v. 18). He asked that they pray that he may be able to be with them soon (v. 19). Their prayer should be that any obstacle to his being with them be removed.

Prayer for the Hebrews that They May be Complete Doing God's Will (vv. 20-21)

The author now shares the prayer he offers for the Hebrews. His prayer is that God, who raised Jesus from the dead and made him the great Shepherd of the sheep (through the blood of the covenant)[14], would make them complete.[15] Being complete, they would be doing God's will (v. 21). The New Covenant is here called the everlasting or eternal covenant (v. 21).

Final Remarks (vv. 22-25)

Verse 21 is the actual end of the letter. The author adds some personal and final remarks.

Heed exhortations (v. 22). The writer urges them to bear patiently with the exhortation he has written giving heed to the warnings that he has written in few words.[16]

---

11 The principle would certainly apply beyond Jerusalem. The world we live in is not continuing or abiding. Rather we are seeking such a city.

12 We must do more than serve God with our lips, we must honor him with our actions and possessions.

13 Sharing with others what we have – benevolence.

14 Commentators differ over whether the phrase "through the blood of the everlasting covenant" qualifies Jesus being brought up from the dead and made the great Shepherd (v. 20) or "make you complete" (v. 21). While it could apply to either, it seems to refer to being raised and made the great Shepherd because the blood he shed was the means by which the New Covenant was ratified.

15 The word translated complete is used of "mending" the nets (Matt. 4:21) and "perfect" what is lacking (1 Thess. 3:10). This reminded them that there is some growing and maturing needed (cf. Heb. 5:11-14; 6).

16 The subjects dealt with in this book could be developed more fully.

Timothy is set free (v. 23). At some point Timothy had been in prison and is now set free. The author hopes to see him.

Salutations to the Hebrews from those in Italy (v. 24). Greetings are sent from the author to the elders and all the saints. Brethren from Italy send greetings as well.

Grace unto them (v. 25). The book closes with a desire for God's grace to be upon them.

Use of the Old Testament in this Chapter	
Verse in Chapter 13	Old Testament Reference
v. 5	Deut. 31:6; Josh. 1:5; 1 Chron. 28:20
v. 6	Psalm 27:1; 118:6

Questions

1. In the context, what are some ways brotherly love can be shown?

2. What can be learned from Abraham entertaining angels, though at the time he was unaware (v.2)?

3. How does remembering those in prison relate to the context?

4. What does verse 4 teach us about the sexual relationship?

5. How does one learn to be content (v. 5)?

6. What practical lesson about leadership do you learn from verse 7?

7. What is the point about Christ being unchangeable (v. 8)?

8. How can we let the elders do their work with joy and not grief (v. 17)?

9. What was the writer's prayer for the Hebrews?

10. What has impressed you most about the book of Hebrews?

CPSIA information can be obtained
at www.ICGtesting.com
Printed in the USA
FSHW012042230719
60298FS